320.973

ANNUAL UPDATE 2016

US GOVERNMENT & POLITICS

Anthony J. Bennett

Philip Allan, an imprint of Hodder Education, an Hachette UK company, Blenheim Court, George Street, Banbury, Oxfordshire OX16 5BH

Orders

Bookpoint Ltd, 130 Park Drive, Milton Park, Abingdon, Oxfordshire OX14 4SE
tel: 01235 827827
fax: 01235 400401
e-mail: education@bookpoint.co.uk

Lines are open 9.00 a.m.–5.00 p.m., Monday to Saturday, with a 24-hour message answering service. You can also order through www.hoddereducation.co.uk

ISBN 978-1-4718-6797-2

First printed 2016

Impression number 5 4 3 2 1

Year 2017 2016

Typeset by Integra Software Services Pvt. Ltd., Pondicherry, India

Cover photo: Kevin Smart/iStock

Printed by CPI Group (UK) Ltd, Croydon, CR0 4YY

Hachette UK's policy is to use papers that are natural, renewable and recyclable products and made from wood grown in sustainable forests. The logging and manufacturing processes are expected to conform to the environmental regulations of the country of origin.

Contents

Chapter 1

Which is healthier — the Democrats or the Republicans?

This chapter updates material on political parties in Chapter 3 of the textbook (Anthony J. Bennett, *A2 US Government and Politics*, 4th edition, 2013).

After almost every set of national elections, political pundits pontificate about the relative health of the two major parties. Such punditry is often contradictory. So, for example, when in 2012 the Republicans lost the popular vote for the fifth time in six presidential elections, commentators consigned them to the ash heap of history, suggesting they were a party a few years away from extinction on the national scene. Two years later, however, the Republicans were winning control of both houses of Congress. So after the 2014 elections it was the Democrats who were having their obituary written — at least as far as congressional elections were concerned. So which party is in the healthier state — the Democrats or the Republicans? The answer is somewhat more complex than the biennial punditry so far referred to would suggest. But first, what *is* the current state of the two parties?

The current state of the parties

We need to give that question a series of answers. As far as *the presidency* is concerned, the Democrats are clearly very healthy, having won the popular vote in five of the past six elections. They actually won the White House in four of those races — 1992, 1996, 2008 and 2012. In 2000 they won the popular vote but lost in the Electoral College. The only presidential election in which they have lost the popular vote in the last 24 years was in 2004, when George W. Bush beat John Kerry by 50.7% to 48.3% — less than 3 percentage points. As Table 1.1 shows, over this period, the Democrats have averaged 48.8% of the popular vote with the Republicans on just 44.9%. Although one of the reasons for the small field of Democratic presidential candidates in 2016 is the presence of Hillary Clinton, the other is the very small base of talented candidates that the party currently possesses.

So what about *Congress*? Here the Republicans are currently in the ascendancy, holding 54 seats in the Senate (to the Democrats' 44, plus 2 independents) and 247 seats in the House (to the Democrats' 188). Thus the Republicans enjoy an 8-seat majority in the Senate and a 59-seat majority in the House. Indeed, the Republicans' 247 seats in the House are more than they have held at any time since 1929 — a truly historic achievement. Between 1993 and 2016, whilst the

Table 1.1 Popular vote by party, 1992–2012

Year	Democrat % of popular vote	Republican % of popular vote
1992	43.0	37.5
1996	49.2	40.7
2000	48.4	47.9
2004	48.3	50.7
2008	52.9	45.7
2012	51.1	47.2
Average	48.8	44.9

party control of the Senate has been pretty evenly divided — the Republicans being the majority party for 12½ years to the Democrats' 11½ years — in the House the Republicans have been in control for 18 of those 24 years. Table 1.2 shows that during this period the Democrats suffered a net loss of 70 House seats, from 258 to just 188.

Table 1.2 House seats by party, 1993–2015

Congress	Democrats in House	Republicans in House
103rd (1993–95)	258	176
104th (1995–97)	204	230
105th (1997–99)	206	228
106th (1999–2001)	211	223
107th (2001–03)	211	221
108th (2003–05)	205	229
109th (2005–07)	201	232
110th (2007–09)	233	202
111th (2009–11)	256	178
112th (2011–13)	193	242
113th (2013–15)	200	233
114th (2015–17)	188	247

Note: Figures are for the start of each Congress.

So at the federal level, the presidency can be scored for the Democrats and the House for the Republicans with the Senate as a draw. But there is a lot more to American politics than what goes on at either end of Pennsylvania Avenue in Washington DC. We need also to find out how the parties are doing around the 50 states. Let's look at the state of play following the 2014 midterm elections. In the *state governorships*, the Republicans control 31 to the Democrats' 18, with Bill Walker of Alaska governing as an independent. Back in 1992, the figures were the complete opposite — 30 Democrats and 18 Republicans, with 2 independents. So here again the Republicans are booming. Indeed on only three occasions — 1929, 1970 and 1997 — have the Republicans held more governorships, holding 32 on those three occasions.

What about the *state legislatures*? The Republicans control 68 of the 98 partisan state legislative chambers with the Democrats controlling just 30. Furthermore, the Republicans control both chambers in 31 states — an all-time record high. Back in 1992 they controlled both chambers in just 8 states. The Democrats, on the other hand, control both chambers in just 11 states — down from 25 in 1992. In terms of legislative seats across the 49 states that have partisan state legislatures (Nebraska has a non-partisan unicameral legislature), following the 2014 midterms the Republicans held 4,124 seats to the Democrats' 3,172. As Figure 1.1 shows, this marks a significant change even within a 6-year period. In 23 states, the Republicans control the state governorship and both houses of the legislature. The Democrats have that overall control in just 7 states.

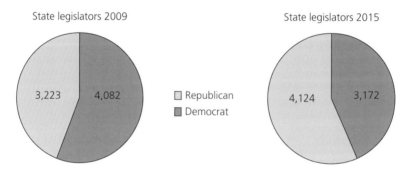

Figure 1.1 Party control of state legislative seats: 2009 and 2015 compared

Here's another telling statistic. Since President Obama was elected in 2009, 85 of the 98 partisan state legislative chambers have become more Republican, 4 have seen no change, and only 9 have become more Democrat. That is a very significant strengthening of the Republican Party at the state level. It will also have an impact on the ability of the Democrats to recruit strong congressional candidates in the coming decade. According to the *Washington Post*'s Dan Balz, 'a serious problem for the Democrats is the drubbing they've taken in the states, the breeding ground for future national talent and for policy experimentation'.

So in terms of current political strength and numerical strength in the shape of office holders, the Republicans are in a much stronger position than the Democrats — a fact which one would hardly discern from contemporary comment in the media. Remember, too, that state governorships are a significant recruitment pool for the presidency, and state legislatures play a similar role for Congress. This bodes well for the Republicans in the coming election cycles. So having considered the current state of both parties, let's look at the problems they face — first at the problems faced by both parties, and then at those faced by the two parties individually.

Table 1.3 Summary of state of parties, 2015

	Democrats	Republicans
Presidency	In power for 16 of the last 24 years Won the popular vote in 5 of last 6 elections	In power for 8 of the last 24 years Won the popular vote in 1 of last 6 elections
Senators	44	54
House members	188	247
State governors	18	31
State legislative chambers	30	68
State legislatures	11	30
State legislators	3,172	4,124
State governments	7	23

Problems facing both parties

There are six problems that we can identify facing both the two major parties.

Few competitive states left in the presidential race

Gone are the days when most of the states were truly competitive in the presidential race. In 1964, Democrat Lyndon Johnson won 44 states. Just 20 years later, Republican Ronald Reagan won 49 states. But that's all changed. In the six presidential elections between 1992 and 2012, 31 states voted for the same party in all six elections — 18 plus the District of Columbia for the Democrats, commanding, in today's money, 242 Electoral College votes; 13 for the Republicans with 102 electoral votes. That's just short of two-thirds of the Electoral College votes accounted for, with only 194 still in play. If one looks at just the last four elections, 45 states have voted for the same party in all four elections — 21 for the Democrats and 24 for the Republicans — leaving only 5 states with 75 Electoral College votes as truly competitive (see Figure 1.2). Thus you could argue that the presidential election of 2016 will be decided in Nevada, Colorado, Ohio, Virginia and Florida — the 5 remaining 'swing' states. Ohio has now elected the winner in all of the last 13 elections — from Johnson in 1964 to Obama in 2012. That's quite a record.

But this creates a significant problem for both parties. The Republicans know that they have little realistic chance today of winning states like California, Pennsylvania, New Jersey or Illinois. That means virtually writing off their 109 Electoral College votes. Yet all those four states were won by George H. W. Bush for the Republicans in 1988. Likewise, the Democrats had better write off Texas, Alabama, South Carolina and Oklahoma with their 63 Electoral College votes. It means that both parties have far fewer possible winning scenarios than they did two or three decades ago.

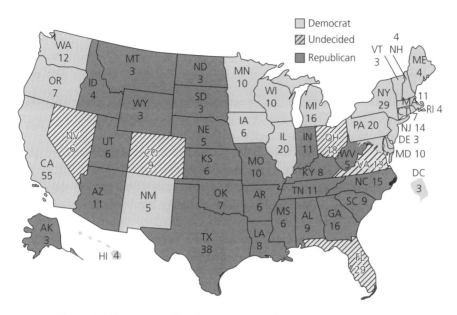

Figure 1.2 States won by the same party in each election, 2000–12

States have become increasingly partisan strongholds

This follows on from our first problem. Today the vast majority of senators come from the same party as the candidate who won their home state in the last two presidential elections. Back in January 1975 just 6 states had been won by the same party at both previous presidential elections and had both senators from the same party. As Table 1.4 shows, this figure had increased to 34 by January 2015.

Table 1.4 State won by the same party in last two presidential elections and with both senators from the same party: 1975 and 2015 compared

January 1975	January 2015	
Arizona (R)	Alabama (R)	Mississippi (R)
Kansas (R)	Alaska (R)	Nebraska (R)
Nevada (R)	Arizona (R)	New Jersey (D)
Oklahoma (R)	Arkansas (R)	New Mexico (D)
Oregon (R)	California (D)	New York (D)
Tennessee (R)	Connecticut (D)	Oklahoma (R)
	Delaware (D)	Oregon (D)
	Georgia (R)	Rhode Island (D)
	Hawaii (D)	South Carolina (R)
	Idaho (R)	South Dakota (R)
	Kansas (R)	Tennessee (R)
	Kentucky (R)	Texas (R)
	Louisiana (R)	Utah (R)
	Maryland (D)	Vermont (D)
	Massachusetts (D)	Virginia (D)
	Michigan (D)	Washington (D)
	Minnesota (D)	Wyoming (R)

The effect of this is to increase the partisanship within both parties in the Senate. The Senate used to be specifically known for its bipartisan compromise and cross-party cooperation. But under today's set-up, there is very little incentive for those 68 senators to work with colleagues from a party that has recently enjoyed so little support within their state — and every incentive to avoid such cooperation, lest it be seen as political treachery and 'rewarded' with a challenger in the next election cycle's primary.

Fewer competitive districts in the House of Representatives

Much the same kind of thing has happened in the House, where the number of competitive districts has declined over the past two decades. A competitive district is one which was won at the previous election by less than 10 percentage points: in other words, one that was no larger than a 54–45% win. Following the 1992 elections, 111 House members were elected in competitive races. By 2004 that figure had fallen to just 31. Although, as Figure 1.3 shows, the number of competitive House districts did rise again over the next three election cycles — back up to 108 by 2010 — the figure had fallen back to 43 in the 2014 midterms.

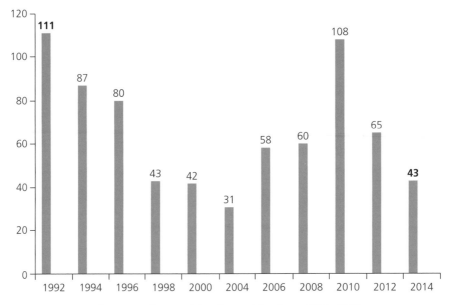

Figure 1.3 Competitive House Districts, 1992–2014

Therefore, as we move towards the 2016 House elections, there are only 43 incumbents who won their seats by less than 10 percentage points. That gives very little opportunity for the Republicans to increase their majority or for Democrats to narrow their minority status. Indeed, on this point, the news is bleaker for Democrats because of those 43 competitive districts, only 19 are held by Republicans. Even if the Democrats were to win all 19, it would still leave them 11 seats short of a majority.

Fewer split districts

Another measure of partisan voting at election time is the number of split districts in the House. A split district is one which votes for a House member of a different party from the candidate who won the district in the presidential race. In 2012, there were 17 districts that voted for Obama in the presidential race but elected a Republican to the House (so-called 'Obama Republicans') and 9 districts that voted for Romney but elected a House Democrat (so-called 'Romney Democrats'). That means that after those elections there were just 26 split districts. Four years earlier there had been 83, and after the 1984 elections there were 196 — over 45% of the total. This very significant decline in split districts is illustrated in Figure 1.4.

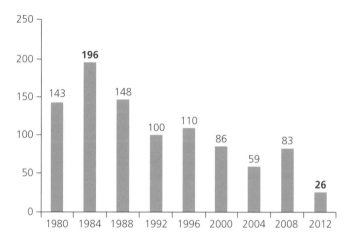

Figure 1.4 Number of split districts, 1980–2012

Given the first two points we made above, this is bad news for both parties. If states and districts are pretty much fixed in a pattern of how they vote in presidential elections, and voting for the House tends to mirror presidential voting, then there is very limited opportunity for either party to make significant inroads into 'enemy territory', especially in a presidential election year such as 2016.

Both parties have low 'favourables'

As Figures 1.5 and 1.6 (page 8) show, both major parties have a huge problem with the way they are viewed by ordinary Americans. By mid-2015, both had unfavourable ratings over 50% and favourable ratings in the 30s. The Republicans have failed to achieve a higher favourable than unfavourable rating for nearly five years whilst the Democrats' favourability rating went over 50% for only the briefest of periods around the time of President Obama's re-election in 2012 — reaching just 51%.

Both parties' leading contenders for 2016 have high negatives

It's not just the parties as a whole that are unpopular. So are the leading contenders in the 2016 presidential race. In the last poll published before her formal declaration, Hillary Clinton's favourability rating stood at 51% with 45% unfavourable. Just four months into her campaign, her favourability rating was down to 37% and her unfavourable rating up to 48%. On the Republican side,

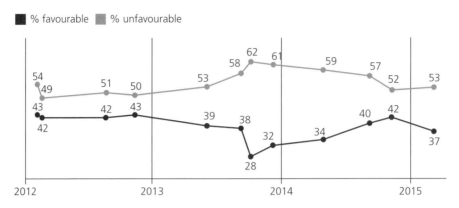

Figure 1.5 Americans' views of the Republican Party, 2012–15

Source: www.gallup.com

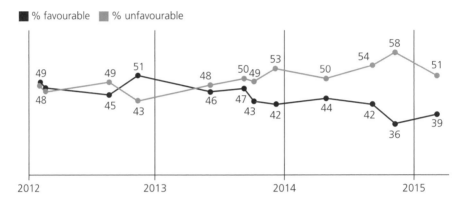

Figure 1.6 Americans' views of the Democratic Party, 2012–15

Source: www.gallup.com

Bush, Huckabee, Cruz, Christie, Trump and Rubio all had overall unfavourable ratings ranging from 1 percentage point for Rubio, to 11 points for Bush, and 32 points for Trump. Neither party's leading candidates were regarded in a favourable light by potential voters.

Problems facing the Democrats

But the Democrats also face four specific problems of their own.

Barack Obama

At first glance, it may seem odd to suggest that President Obama is a problem to the Democrats going into 2016. After all, he's the one person we know definitely won't be on the ballot on 8 November. But to see how Obama can still be a drag on the Democrats this year, one has only to remember the effect that outgoing presidents Ronald Reagan, Bill Clinton and George W. Bush had in 1988, 2000 and 2008 respectively. The simplest way to understand this effect is to conduct what I call the TV Debate Test by asking the question, 'Who will be mentioning President Obama during the 2016 presidential debates later this year?'

Eight years ago, outgoing president George W. Bush was mentioned 27 times during the TV debates between Democrat Barack Obama and Republican John McCain. Obama mentioned Bush 21 times, whilst McCain mentioned him only 6 times. Conclusion: unpopular Bush was a drag on the Republican ticket and hence McCain avoided too many mentions, whilst Obama was happy to keep on dropping in his name.

It was the same eight years earlier in the 2000 election. Outgoing president Bill Clinton chalked up 14 mentions during the Bush–Gore debates with 13 of those mentions coming from Bush. Gore, who had served eight years as Clinton's vice-president, mentioned him only once during three debates. He knew that the mention of Clinton's name was a negative for his campaign.

But back in 1988, it was all quite different. Outgoing president Ronald Reagan got 21 mentions during the debates between Democrat Michael Dukakis and Republican George H. W. Bush — Reagan's vice-president. This time 18 of those mentions came from Bush; only 3 from Dukakis. Bush knew that mentioning Reagan's name was a huge plus for his campaign.

So what about 2016? Will the Democrat be happy or reluctant to mention Obama? Will it be 1988 again, or will it be 2000 and 2008? My hunch — and it's only that — is that you will hear more about Obama from the Republicans than from the Democrats in 2016. And that's why Obama — the man who won the Democrats the last two elections — has the potential to be a drag on the ticket this time around.

Reid and Pelosi

Not only do the Democrats have a problem with their White House occupant, they also have two more problems on Capitol Hill. As Table 1.5 shows, the Democrats' congressional leaders in both the Senate and the House — Harry Reid of Nevada and Nancy Pelosi of California — have low favourables and high unfavourables. Neither is regarded as an electoral asset. Both have presided over the loss of the majority in their respective chambers — Reid in 2014 and Pelosi in 2010. Indeed, Pelosi has now led the House Democrats to defeat in three successive elections. Both are 76 years of age. Both are seen as well beyond their sell-by dates. As a consequence the Democrats have a problem with tired and discredited congressional leadership.

Table 1.5 Reid and Pelosi: favourable/unfavourable ratings

	Favourable	Unfavourable
Senate Minority Leader Harry Reid	22%	45%
House Minority Leader Nancy Pelosi	27%	52%

Source: http://elections.huffingtonpost.com/pollster

The 'socialist' wing

It is likely that the campaign of Bernie Sanders to win the Democrats' 2016 presidential nomination will expose what one might describe as the 'socialist' wing of the party. Despite the centralising effect of Bill Clinton (1993–2001) and to some extent Barack Obama, there is still within the Democratic Party a left-wing rump that resents the 'New Democrat' reform of the party that Bill Clinton masterminded in the 1990s. Sanders began his political life in the Liberty Union Party — an anti-war socialist party. He has been in Congress since 1990 and has always sat as an independent who caucuses with the Democrats. Although Sanders represents a minority view within the Democratic Party, his presidential campaign may well force Hillary Clinton to tack further to the left in the primaries, making it more difficult for her to appeal to the middle ground in the general election, were she to be nominated.

The South

Today, the South — with its 182 Electoral College votes — is critical in any presidential election. Those southern electoral votes account for more than two-thirds of the 270 required to win the White House. Yet in the last four elections the Democrats have won in only three states — Florida and Virginia twice (2008 and 2012), and North Carolina once (2008). In both 2000 and 2004, they lost all 11 southern states. Even running with two southerners — Bill Clinton of Arkansas and Al Gore of Tennessee — in 1992 and 1996, the Democrats lost the South on both occasions. Indeed, the last time the Democrats won the South in a presidential election was 40 years ago — and that was with a southern candidate, Jimmy Carter, in 1976. As the Democrats have no true southerners running in 2016, it seems that most — if not all — of those 182 Electoral College votes could once again end up in the Republican column. That's a big deficit for the Democrats to overcome.

Problems facing the Republicans

But the Republicans face some problems of their own.

George W. Bush

In February 2010, drivers on Interstate 35 passing through the town of Wyoming in eastern Minnesota were amused to see a huge roadside billboard bearing a picture of a smiling and waving George W. Bush with the caption 'Missing Me Yet?' Just over a year into the Obama presidency, a group of local business executives had paid for the billboard, thinking that others like them would answer the question with a resounding 'yes'. However, polling data between 2009 and 2014 suggested that most Americans answered the question in the negative. Certainly Bush was still a drag on the Republican ticket in 2012.

But Figure 1.7 might show some light at the end of the tunnel for Republicans, with the *Washington Post* reporting in June 2015 that the former president now has better ratings than the former first lady Hillary Clinton. Were Bush's brother Jeb to be the 2016 Republican nominee, it would be very important that the Bush brand was not still regarded as toxic.

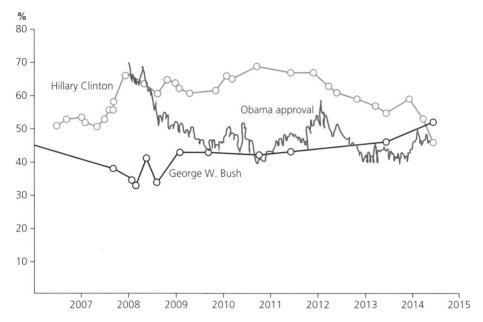

%

80 —

70 —

60 — Hillary Clinton

Obama approval

50 —

40 — George W. Bush

30 —

20 —

10 —

2007   2008   2009   2010   2011   2012   2013   2014   2015

Figure 1.7 Favourability ratings of Bush, Clinton and Obama compared, 2007–15

Source: www.washingtonpost.com

McConnell and Boehner

For much of the last six years, the Republicans have also had their own problems on Capitol Hill in the shape of Senate Majority Leader Mitch McConnell of Kentucky and former House Speaker John Boehner (pronounced 'Bay-ner') of Ohio. Indeed, if you thought Reid and Pelosi's figures were bad, those for the Republican leadership duo were even worse (Table 1.6). Although both had the advantage of having led their party to victory in recent elections, they were both viewed as somewhat flawed leaders. Neither cut a dashing figure of youth and vitality — McConnell is 74 and Boehner a chain-smoking 65.

Table 1.6 McConnell and Boehner: favourable/unfavourable ratings

	Favourable	Unfavourable
Senate Majority Leader Mitch McConnell	19%	48%
House Speaker John Boehner	20%	53%

Source: http://elections.huffingtonpost.com/pollster

But then in September 2014, Boehner suddenly announced his resignation from both the speakership and the House, effectively forced out of the Speaker's office by a powerful group of ultra-conservative House Republicans known collectively as the House Freedom Caucus. The same group even managed to force House Majority Leader Kevin McCarthy out of the race to succeed Boehner.

The 'fruitcake' wing

One could call this the Tea Party wing, but as fruitcake in the edible sense is a popular ingredient of any tea party, I'm also using the term here in its informal sense (see below). The Republicans' fruitcake wing would not only include Tea Party activists and their preferred candidates but could be easily extended to include Donald Trump — the political bull with the portable china shop.

Fruitcake (*n.*)

1 a cake containing dried fruit and nuts.
2 *informal,* an eccentric or mad person.

As with Sanders in the Democratic Party, it is unlikely that any so-described Republican will land the nomination, but they could push the nominee to the right in the primaries and even affect the writing of the party platform later in the year. This would repeat the problems that Mitt Romney faced in his 2012 general election campaign, when he was defending policies well to his right that he didn't really believe in himself.

Women

Democrats have their problems in the South; Republicans have their problems with women. It is now over 30 years — Ronald Reagan in 1984 — since a Republican presidential candidate won the women's vote. In that year, Reagan won 56% of women's votes to 44% for his Democrat opponent Walter Mondale. But in the subsequent seven elections, the Democrats have averaged over 52% of the vote amongst women to just 43% for the Republicans. That 9 percentage point gap is a significant reason why the Republicans have won the popular vote in only two of those seven elections. Furthermore, the Republicans may face an even bigger challenge in 2016 — how to compete for women's votes against a female Democratic candidate.

Conclusions

We can see from this survey that both parties have their strengths and weaknesses. The Democrats appear to be in a much stronger position in the presidential race whilst the Republicans are healthier in congressional and state elections. But what will this mean for 2016? The health of each party by the year's end will probably depend on the answers to the following four questions:

1 Which party will choose the most politically attractive candidate?

2 Which party will pursue policies in which the electorate is most interested?

3 Which party's candidate will run the most effective campaign?

4 Which voters will turn out on Election Day?

Upon the answers to these four questions will hang the health of America's two major parties in 2016.

Questions

1 What do Tables 1.1 and 1.2 tell us about the current state of the two parties?
2 To what extent are the Republicans currently stronger than the Democrats in state politics?
3 What problem is created for both parties by the lack of competitive states in presidential elections?
4 What do Table 1.4 and Figures 1.3 and 1.4 tell us about the partisan state of the Senate and the House?
5 What problems for both parties do Figures 1.5 and 1.6 illustrate?
6 In what way may President Obama be a problem for the Democrats in 2016?
7 What other problems does the Democratic Party currently face?
8 What problems face the Republican Party?
9 So which do you think is healthier, the Democrats or the Republicans? (Give your reasons.)

Chapter 2

Women in US politics: how much have things changed?

How times change. Forty years ago, in 1976, no major party had fielded a woman on its presidential ticket. There were no women in the United States Senate and just 19 in the House of Representatives — that's just 4% of the total membership. The United States Supreme Court was still five years away from gaining its first female justice. President Ford had just appointed the first woman to the president's cabinet for over 30 years. So it seems a good moment — in the year when America could elect its first woman president — to take stock of the significant changes in women's representation that have taken place in both national and state politics.

But before we do, it is worth asking the question, 'Why is any of this important? Does it matter if women are not equally represented in politics and government?' The short answer is 'Yes, it does matter' — and for two significant reasons. First, equal representation of men and women in politics and government upholds the democratic values of fairness and representative government. To quote Bill Clinton from 1992, America's government should 'look like America'. And second, it has significant policy implications. Academic studies have shown that women in government are much more likely to raise and tackle issues concerning civil rights and liberties, education, health and the workplace than are men.

Women in presidential politics

In an interview in *Rolling Stone* magazine in September 2015, Donald Trump said this about his fellow Republican presidential hopeful Carly Fiorina:

> Look at that face. Would anyone vote for that? Can you imagine that, the face of our next president?

Trump later tried some damage limitation by saying that he had been talking about Ms Fiorina's 'persona', not her appearance. When Trump's comments were put to Fiorina in a late-September Republican presidential debate by moderator Jake Tapper, Fiorina replied:

> You know, it's interesting to me. Mr Trump said that he heard Mr [Jeb] Bush very clearly and what Mr Bush said. I think women all over this country heard very clearly what Mr Trump said.

In 1964 Senator Margaret Chase Smith, a Republican from Maine, became the first woman to have her name placed in nomination for president at a major party's convention. When she declared her candidacy in January of that year, she remarked: 'I have few illusions and no money, but I'm staying for the finish.' She lost every primary, but did manage a very respectable 25% of the vote in Illinois. In the convention ballot, she received just 27 votes, as against 883 for the winner, Senator Barry Goldwater. It would be another 36 years before a Republican woman ran for the presidency.

Meanwhile, as shown in Table 2.1, the Democrats had two women running in the 1972 presidential primaries, but only Shirley Chisholm, a black congresswoman from New York, made it all the way to the convention, where she finished fourth in the balloting with 152 votes (5%).

The 1984 election did see the first woman nominated for the vice presidency by a major party with Democrat Walter Mondale choosing Representative Geraldine Ferraro of New York as his running-mate. But they lost to the Republican ticket of Ronald Reagan and George H. W. Bush by 525 Electoral College votes to 13, winning just one state. The Mondale–Ferraro ticket even lost amongst women voters by 12 percentage points!

In 1987, Colorado congresswoman Patricia Schroeder announced she was running for the following year's Democratic nomination but pulled out of the race in September of the same year, months even before the first primary. This was the same year in which British prime minister Margaret Thatcher won her third consecutive general election for the Conservative Party. But in the United States by the dawn of the twenty-first century, only two women had made it to the nominating convention of a major party, and the most recent was by then almost 30 years distant.

Table 2.1 Women major party presidential candidates, 1964–2012

Year	Candidate	Party	Progress
1964	**Margaret Chase-Smith**	R	**27 votes at convention**
1972	**Shirley Chisholm**	D	**152 votes at convention**
	Patsy Mink	D	Withdrew May 1972
1988	Patricia Schroeder	D	Withdrew September 1987
2000	Elizabeth Dole	R	Withdrew October 1999
2004	Carol Moseley Braun	D	Withdrew January 2004
2008	**Hillary Rodham Clinton**	D	Won primaries in 21 states
			1,010 votes at convention
2012	Michele Bachmann	R	Withdrew January 2012

Note: Those who reached the convention are shown in bold.

The first two elections of the new century were no more promising for women candidates in either party. Republican Elizabeth Dole, wife of the party's 1996 nominee Bob Dole, announced she was running for the party's nomination in 2000 but, woefully short of money, she pulled out of the race well before the primaries started. In the summer of 2000 she was mentioned as a possible vice-presidential choice for George W. Bush, but Bush went for Dick Cheney instead. Four years later Democrat Carol Moseley Braun did little better, dropping out four days before the nomination contest officially opened with the Iowa caucuses.

So when on 8 January 2008, Hillary Clinton won the Democrats' New Hampshire primary by 3 percentage points over Barack Obama, this was the first time that a woman had won a presidential primary. It is extraordinary to think that this happened just eight years ago and shows how long and hard was the road for women to be successful in presidential politics. Clinton had begun the nominating cycle as the odds-on favourite. She had herself predicted that the Democratic race would be 'all over by February 5' — with her as the winner. Instead, on that day (Super Tuesday), she won only 9 of the 22 state contests. Although she went on to win further victories in some big states, she was by this time too far behind in the delegate count to have any realistic chance of winning the nomination. She ploughed on to the final primaries in early June but it was by then a lost cause. With delegates now deserting her for the putative nominee Barack Obama, she pressed on to the convention where she won less than a quarter of the delegate votes. Because early expectations had been so high, what had really been a great achievement now looked like abject failure. So it was not the Democrats who had a woman on their presidential ticket in 2008 but the Republicans, when John McCain made the surprise choice of Alaska governor Sarah Palin to be his running-mate. But the ticket lost badly in November.

Four years later there was no evidence of the 'Clinton effect' in advancing the cause of women in presidential politics. The Republicans had a large field of candidates to challenge President Obama's bid for a second term, but only one was a woman — Minnesota congresswoman Michele Bachmann. Bachmann shot to early prominence when she won the Iowa Straw Poll in August 2011, the first woman to do so. But when in January 2012 the state's Republicans held their presidential caucuses, Bachmann finished sixth with less than 5% of the vote and immediately withdrew from the race.

It's against that background that Hillary Clinton launched her second presidential bid and former Hewlett-Packard CEO Carly Fiorina announced herself a candidate in the Republican race. By the time you read this chapter, you will have a much better feel for how those two candidacies will pan out. Will 2016 be the Year of the Woman in US presidential politics or will it be just another year of (male) business as usual?

Women in Congress

It is exactly 100 years since the first woman — Jeannette Rankin, a Republican from Montana — was elected to Congress. In January 2015, of the 535 members of Congress, 104 (or 19%) of them were women. Of those 104, 20 were in the Senate and 84 in the House, 76 were Democrats and 28 were Republicans. In the past 100 years, 307 women have been elected to Congress, with California leading the way with 39 followed by New York with 27. Three states — Delaware, Mississippi and Vermont — have never sent a woman to Congress. It wasn't until 1978 that the first woman was elected to the Senate without having previously filled an unexpired term of another senator. That was Republican Nancy Kassebaum of Kansas. Figure 2.1 shows that the number of women in Congress has increased steadily over the past 25 years, and although the rate of increase slowed during the first decade of this century, the elections of 2012 and 2014 saw further increases.

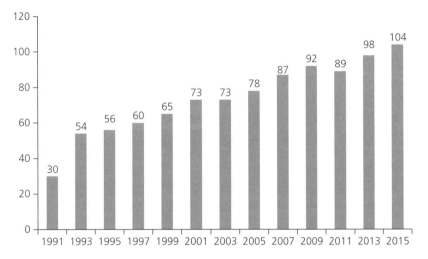

Figure 2.1 Women in Congress, 1991–2015

It is, of course, inevitable that the number of women elected to Congress will largely reflect the number of women who are nominated as congressional candidates — in winnable seats. Figure 2.2 shows the number of women candidates standing in both House and Senate elections since 1990. The jump in women candidates in 1992 from 77 to 117 led to an increase in women members from 30 to 54 led to an increase in women members from 30 to 54 (see Figure 2.1). (1992 was the year that the Democrats entitled ' The year of the woman'.) But whereas the number of women candidates during this 26-year period has increased just over two-fold, the number of women in Congress has increased more than three-fold.

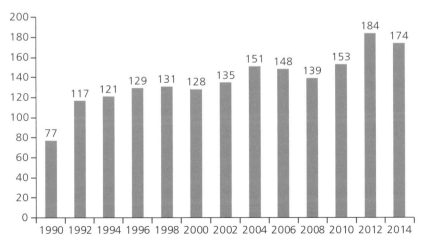

Figure 2.2 Women candidates for Congress, 1990–2014

There are probably two reasons for this. First, as more women stood and were elected, the idea of women being elected to Congress became more acceptable. Gone was the bumper sticker seen back in the 1990s, 'A woman's place is in the home, not in the House'. Second, parties — and particularly the Democrats — started to nominate women in winnable and competitive seats. Of the 174 women who stood for Congress in 2014, 119 (68%) were Democrats, and of the 104 who were elected, 76 (73%) were Democrats. As this was a year in which the Republicans were in the ascendancy, it would suggest that Democrats are more likely to choose women in genuinely winnable seats than are the Republicans.

To what extent are women included in congressional leadership? With the Democrats currently in the minority in both houses, there are far fewer women in leadership posts in Congress than was the case during those years when the Democrats were the majority party, between 2007 and 2011. At that time even the Speaker of the House was a woman — Nancy Pelosi. Currently, Ms Pelosi is House Minority Leader. The Republican House leadership is entirely male, though there are two women Republicans serving as whips.

Box 2.1 Women within the Senate Democratic leadership

Chief Deputy Whip: Barbara Boxer (California)

Caucus Secretary: Patty Murray (Washington)

Policy Committee Vice-Chair: Debbie Stabenow (Michigan)

Policy Committee Strategic Policy Adviser: Elizabeth Warren (Massachusetts)

Steering and Outreach Chair: Amy Klobuchar (Minnesota)

Steering and Outreach Vice-Chair: Jeanne Shaheen (New Hampshire)

As Box 2.1 shows, in the Senate the Democrats have appointed six of their 14 women to leadership posts. But the representation of women in terms of the chairing of congressional committees is truly abysmal. Only one of the Senate's 16 standing committees is currently chaired by a women — Energy and Natural Resources, chaired by Lisa Murkowski of Alaska — and only one of 21 House committees — House Administration, by Candice Miller of Michigan. Neither committee ranks in the list of the most prestigious or powerful within Congress. Six of the 16 committees in the Senate have a woman as Ranking Member (that is, the senior Democrat), and a further six in the House.

Women in the federal executive

Having considered the rise of women in elective politics at the federal level, what about in appointive posts? If we look back just over 50 years to the Kennedy administration in 1961, there have been 234 people appointed to head what are now the 15 executive departments of the federal government. The heads of these departments make up the regular membership of the president's cabinet. During these 56 years — from Kennedy to Obama — of those 234 people, 30 (13%) were women. But if we break that period down, we will see that there has been an increase in women at the top of these departments over the past two decades. During the first 32 years (1961–92) there were 142 appointments, of which just 11 (7%) were women. But in the subsequent 24 years (1993–2016) there have been 92 appointments, of which 19 (21%) have been women.

In the 1960s, presidents Kennedy, Johnson and Nixon all appointed all-male cabinets. It was Gerald Ford in 1975 who appointed the first woman to the cabinet since the 1930s, when he chose Carla Hills to be secretary of housing and urban development (HUD). A few years after she left office, I interviewed Ms Hills. She told me:

> I knew the President was looking for someone at HUD. He called me by phone and asked me to go over to the White House, and I met with the President. When he offered me HUD I was surprised as I had no background in urban affairs — nor in housing. I told the President, 'I think you'll have some political flack in nominating me.'

It wasn't only her lack of policy specialism that was controversial. Ford was appointing the first woman to the cabinet for 40 years.

When Jimmy Carter arrived in the White House in 1977, he included two women in his initial cabinet, and when the new Department of Education was formed in 1979, he appointed Shirley Hufstedler to head it up. In 1981, Ronald Reagan reverted to an all-male line-up to lead the federal departments, but he brought in two women later in his first term and another in his second term, though there were never more than two women in the cabinet at any one time. It was much the same with the first George Bush, with Elizabeth Dole at Labor being the only woman at the start. When she left in 1990, she was replaced by Lynn Martin. Two years later Barbara Franklin was appointed to head the Department of Commerce.

When Bill Clinton was elected in 1992, he made a good deal of gender representation in his administration, famously remarking that he wanted a cabinet that 'looked like America'. But of the 14 heads of executive departments, only three were women. What was different was that for the first time a woman was appointed to one of the four top-tier departments with Janet Reno heading up the Department of Justice as Attorney General. At the start of his second term in 1997, Clinton appointed Madeline Albright as the first ever female secretary of state.

In 2005, George W. Bush's second-term cabinet contained four women, including Condoleezza Rice as secretary of state. This number was equalled by Barack Obama in both his first and second terms, including during the first term yet another female secretary of state. Indeed, during a 16-year period between 1997 and 2013, the State Department was headed by a woman for 12 of those years.

Women on the Supreme Court

For 192 years, the United States Supreme Court remained an all-male institution. Right through the 1970s, textbooks would rightly refer to the 'nine old men' on the Court. But that all changed in 1981 with President Reagan's nomination of Sandra Day O'Connor to the nation's highest court. That Reagan should be the president to make such a ground-breaking appointment is certainly surprising. Throughout his 1980 campaign, Reagan had opposed the Equal Rights Amendment to the Constitution — a move that made women reluctant to support his campaign. About three weeks before Election Day, with the polls tightening but President Carter still ahead, Reagan adviser Stuart Spencer felt the Reagan campaign had gone flat and needed a new boost. With no vacancy having occurred on the Supreme Court for five years, Spencer suggested to Governor Reagan that he should announce his intention to appoint the first woman to the Court. Reagan was at first reluctant, but at a news conference in Los Angeles on 14 October Reagan made the announcement (see Box 2.2). It made front-page news in the *New York Times*, which called it 'a bold move'. Carter dismissed it as a cynical gesture, remarking that 'equal rights for women involves more than just one job for one woman'.

Box 2.2 **Ronald Reagan's news conference statement, 14 October 1980**

As you know, a number of false and misleading accusations have been made in this campaign. During the next three weeks, I intend to set the record straight. One of the accusations has been that I am somehow opposed to full and equal opportunities for women in America…I am announcing today that one of the first Supreme Court vacancies in my administration will be filled by the most qualified woman I can find.

Within a few months of Reagan taking office, Supreme Court justice Potter Stewart told Reagan that he intended to retire at the end of the Court's term in late June. The following day, Attorney General William French Smith asked one of his assistants, Ken Starr, to begin research on a list of potential nominees. To get the ball rolling, Smith scrawled a few names on a pink telephone message slip and handed it to Starr. 'Who's O'Connor?' asked Starr. 'All I've got here is a last name.'

Table 2.2 Women appointed to the Supreme Court

Justice	Nominated by	Years on the Court
Sandra Day O'Connor	Ronald Reagan	1981–2006
Ruth Bader Ginsburg	Bill Clinton	1993–
Sonia Sotomayor	Barack Obama	2009–
Elena Kagan	Barack Obama	2010–

Sandra Day O'Connor was in just her second year on the Arizona State Court of Appeals. Her credentials were not obviously those of a Supreme Court nominee, most of whom have served some years on either the federal appeal courts or their state supreme court. At 10 o'clock on 1 July 1981, O'Connor was picked up outside a pharmacy on Dupont Circle, about a mile north of the White House in downtown Washington. Fifteen minutes later she was being ushered into the Oval Office for her first ever meeting with President Reagan. In the next 45 minutes, Reagan made up his mind to appoint O'Connor to the Supreme Court. Six days later, Reagan walked into the White House Briefing Room to make it official — that after 192 years and 101 male justices, the Court was to have its first female member. 'Judge Sandra Day O'Connor's place in history is already secure based on today's announcement that she will be President Reagan's nominee as the first woman on the United States Supreme Court,' front-paged the *New York Times* the following day. Her nearly 25 years of distinguished tenure on the Court cemented that place in history, for whatever you thought of her decisions, she was undoubtedly a justice who made a difference.

By the time O'Connor retired from the Court in January 2006, she had been joined by Clinton appointee Ruth Bader Ginsburg, and President Obama would appoint two more women to the Court during his first term to bring the number up to three.

Box 2.3   **The Brethren's first Sister**

The symbolism was stunning. By giving the Brethren their first Sister, Reagan provided not only a breakthrough on the bench but a powerful push forward in the shamefully long and needlessly tortuous march of women toward full equality in American society.

> Ed Magnuson, 'The Brethren's First Sister: A Supreme Court Nominee — and a Triumph for Common Sense,' *Time* magazine, 20 July 1981

Women in state politics

So much for women in Washington, but what has happened around the individual states? Figure 2.3 (page 22) shows the significant increase that occurred in women state governors in just ten years between 1995 and 2005 — from one to nine. In the 24 years between 1991 and 2015, 23 women were elected as state governor, and a further four served having succeeded their predecessor without election. Arizona led the way, electing three consecutive female governors covering an 18-year period: Jane Dee Hull (Republican, 1997–2003), Janet Napolitano (Democrat, 2003–09) and Jan Brewer (Republican, 2009–15). During this same period both Kansas and New Hampshire elected two women governors. And the most high profile? Probably Democrat Ann Richards of Texas (1991–95), who was defeated for a second term by George W. Bush, and of course Republican Sarah Palin of Alaska (2007–09), who was John McCain's controversial running-mate in the 2008 presidential race.

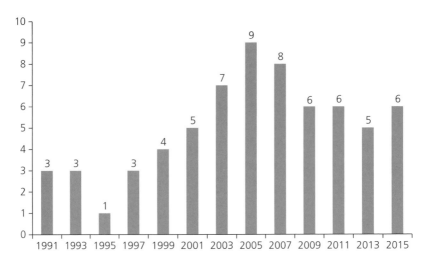

Figure 2.3 Women as state governors, 1991–2015

But by 2015, only six women were serving as state governors: Republicans Mary Fallin of Oklahoma, Nikki Haley of South Carolina and Susana Martinez of New Mexico; Democrats Maggie Hassan of New Hampshire, Gina Raimondo of Rhode Island and Kate Brown of Oregon. The party distribution of women governors has been more even during this period than in Congress with 13 Democrats elected and 10 Republicans.

In the state legislatures following the 2014 elections, women held 1,793 of the 7,383 state legislative seats, which represents 24% of the total. Around 60% are Democrats and just under 40% are Republicans. But there is a wide variation across the states from a high of 42% of women in the Colorado state legislature to a low of 11% in Louisiana. The top ten states are predominantly in the more liberal western half of the country, whilst the bottom ten are predominantly in the more conservative South.

As in Congress, so in the state legislatures the proportion of women has increased over recent decades, as is shown in Figure 2.4. Forty years ago in 1975, just 8% of state legislators were women. Now the figure is just over 24%. But the rate of increase over the past two decades has certainly slowed significantly.

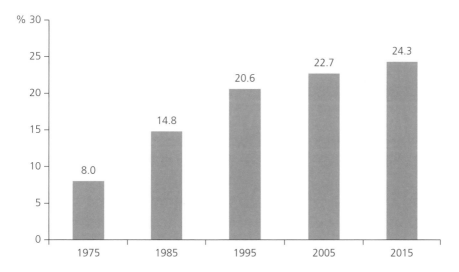

Figure 2.4 Women as a percentage of state legislators, 1975–2015

How much have things changed?

So how much have things changed for women in American politics? As we have seen, there have been some significant increases in the representation of women in all three branches of the federal government as well as in state politics over the past two to three decades. Things have moved on since the 1960s. But there are still significant problems. The pace of change has been modest at best, glacial at worst. As I write this, almost half the states have never had a woman governor, and no major party has selected a woman as its presidential candidate. Women still constitute only around 20% of the membership of Congress. What is more, the graphs in this chapter show a significant slowing in the rates of increase for women at pretty much all levels of government. Progress seems to have reached a plateau.

When one makes international comparisons, the picture is fairly bleak. A study published just two years ago showed that America ranked 98th in the world for the percentage of women in its national legislature, just behind Kenya and Indonesia and only just ahead of the United Arab Emirates. That's embarrassing — the more so as America ranked 59th in the same table back in 1998. Cynthia Terrell, chair of FairVote's 'Representation 2020' project — part of the Center for Voting and Democracy, a pressure group campaigning for electoral reform in the United States — commented that, given the current rate of progress, 'women won't achieve fair representation for nearly 500 years!'

Such change that has occurred can be credited to the work of political parties — especially the Democratic Party — and of pressure groups. It is now 30 years since the interest group EMILY's List was founded in the United States. EMILY is an acronym for Early Money Is Like Yeast — it raises the 'dough'. Back in 1985, EMILY's List was directly involved in the election of Barbara Mikulski as the first Democrat woman to be elected to the United States Senate in her own right. She is now the longest-serving woman in Congress and retires this year after 40 years on Capitol Hill — 10 years in the House and 30 years in the Senate. In 2016, EMILY's List is endorsing Hillary Clinton's bid for the presidency and hopes to raise more than $60 million for pro-choice women candidates. Other groups, though on a smaller scale, exist to promote pro-life and conservative women candidates for federal, state and local offices. Significant work has also been done by the National Organization for Women (NOW) and the Feminist Majority Foundation. But such groups may have taken reform as far as it can go unless other very significant reforms are made.

Ask any political scientist who has studied women's representation issues and they will tell you that if you really want to change the representation of women in national and state politics, then you need to change the systems both of selection and of election. Most countries that have made significant moves towards women's equality in their legislatures have done so through their political parties adopting mandatory quotas for women in the selection of candidates. And as can be seen from Table 2.3, most of those top ten countries in the table of women in national legislatures use a proportional — or mixed — electoral system.

Table 2.3 Women in national legislatures: top ten countries

Rank	Country	Percentage of women		Electoral system(s) used
		Lower House	Upper House	
1	Rwanda	63.8	38.5	PR
2	Andorra	50.0	—	Mixed
3	Cuba	48.9	—	Winner-takes-all
4	Sweden	45.0	—	PR
5	Seychelles	43.8	—	Mixed
6	Senegal	42.7	—	Mixed
7	Finland	42.5	—	PR
8	South Africa	42.3	32.1	PR
9	Nicaragua	40.2	—	PR
10	Iceland	39.7	—	PR

Source: www.representation2020.com/women-in-parliaments.html

Conclusions

Having said that, the likelihood of either of those reforms occurring in the United States is fairly remote. The Constitution does not require a winner-takes-all electoral system operated in single-member constituencies. But electoral reform is certainly not even on the radar of either major political party, or on the policy agenda of most Americans. Shirley Chisholm was the first woman to run for the presidential nomination of the Democratic Party. Ms Chisholm was also an African American. She once famously remarked that 'of my two "handicaps" being female put many more obstacles in my path than being black'. The fact that America had a black president before it had even a female presidential candidate bears out the truth of Chisholm's observation more than 40 years ago.

Questions

1 Why does women's representation in American government and politics matter?
2 Summarise the progress made by women candidates in each major party's presidential race since 1964.
3 What do the data in Figures 2.1 and 2.2 tell us about the number of women in Congress?
4 To what extent are women included in today's congressional leadership?
5 What progress have women made in the top jobs in the federal executive departments?
6 Why was it surprising that it was President Reagan who appointed the first woman to the Supreme Court? When did this occur?
7 Why was Sandra Day O'Connor a surprise selection for that post?
8 What do Figures 2.3 and 2.4 tell us about women in state politics?
9 How does America compare with other countries in women's representation in national legislatures?
10 Which pressure groups have worked for the increase in women's representation in elective offices in the United States?
11 What significant reforms would have to be made to bring about gender equality in elective offices in the United States?

Chapter 3

Where now for televised presidential debates?

What you need to know

- Televised presidential debates during the general election began in 1960 when there were four debates between John Kennedy and Richard Nixon.
- There were then no further debates until 1976 when there were three debates between Gerald Ford and Jimmy Carter, plus the first ever vice presidential debate.
- Presidential and vice presidential debates have been held in each successive election, though the number has varied.
- Different formats have been developed.
- The early debates were sponsored and organised by the League of Women Voters but in 1987 the Commission on Presidential Debates was formed to sponsor, organise and produce all future debates.

This chapter updates material on presidential debates on pages 76–82 of the textbook (Anthony J. Bennett, *A2 US Government and Politics*, 4th edition, 2013).

They seemed like a good idea at the time and they were certainly popular. Millions of Americans tuned in to watch. They were the very best in political theatre. When televised presidential debates first took to the airwaves, it was in the days of flickering black-and-white pictures shown on sets that were as big as a large family-size refrigerator. It was 26 September 1960, and there were Senator Kennedy and Vice President Nixon live on CBS from Chicago. That year there were four debates on three networks with two candidates, each at a podium, and one moderator asking the questions. And what do we remember most about those debates almost six decades ago? Probably that Nixon had a 'five o'clock shadow', was sweating, and looked somewhat shifty in his grey suit that blended into the studio background, and that in contrast Kennedy looked young and handsome, and portrayed a crisp figure in his dark suit. And notice that we remember little or nothing about the substance of the debates. All we talk about is style — or the lack of it.

In the 56 years since then, so much has changed. Of course, the medium of television has changed — now colour, HD, digital and on huge but slender screens. The debate format has changed too, with candidates often sitting around on bar stools, strolling around answering questions asked directly by an invited audience. There have been debates with the candidates sat around a table with the moderator. Sometimes, there's been a panel of moderators. In 1992, there were even three candidates, rather than two. And if you don't want to watch the debate, well there aren't just two other channels from which to choose, but more like two hundred. Yet for all this change, some things remain the same. As we approach the twelfth election cycle in which such debates will have been used during the general election, it's a good moment to ask 'where now for presidential debates?' What's wrong with them, and how could they be improved?

The TV audiences

When the TV debates began, network television dominated the media landscape in America. This was the era of the old media — network television and print media. There just wasn't anything else. There was no Fox News, no CNN, no MSNBC and of course there was no internet or social media. As Table 3.1 shows, the rise of the so-called new media did not even begin until two decades after the first TV debates were aired. Indeed, it probably seems almost unbelievable to most readers that just 12 years ago there was no Facebook, YouTube or Twitter, no iPhones and no iPads. So fast has been the change in the new media that the Blackberry, like the fax machine, has virtually come and gone in less than two decades.

Table 3.1 The rise of the new media

New media operation	Year begun/introduced
CNN	1980
Talk Radio	Early 1990s
Internet	1991
Text messaging	1992
Blogging	1997
Blackberry	1999
Linked In	2003
Facebook	2004
YouTube	2005
Twitter	2006
iPhone	2007
iPad	2010

With this vast plethora of new media it is therefore hardly surprising that viewership of the presidential debates has declined over the decades. There are just so many more means by which to glean news and information about the candidates and the campaign. Traditional media are therefore desperately trying to adapt to a world in which digital content is increasingly the source of campaign information for most Americans. Figure 3.1 (page 28) shows that the percentage of US households viewing the TV debates declined from just under 60% in 1960 to under 20% in both 1996 and 2000, with only a slight recovery during the last three election cycles.

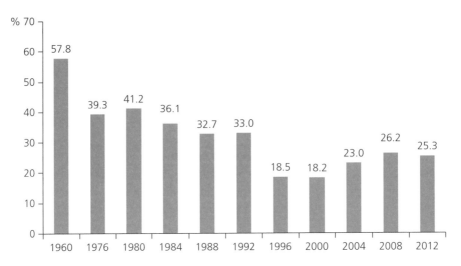

Figure 3.1 Average percentage across all debates of voting age population that watched the presidential and vice presidential debates on television

Source: *Democratising the Debates*, Annenberg Public Policy Center, University of Pennsylvania, 2015

Furthermore, the problem of low TV audiences may become even more marked in future cycles. Research shows a sharp distinction in TV debate viewership between 18–34-year-olds and older voters, with viewership significantly lower amongst the 18–34-year-olds than amongst older voters (see Table 3.2). Amongst those who did watch a debate in 2012, 59% of over-65s watched all of the debate, whereas only 42% of the 18–34 age group did so. This latter age group are more used to getting their political information in 140 characters or from a 'friend' on Facebook than sitting and watching a 90-minute piece of television. Even that length of time — 90 minutes — probably speaks to a very different era.

Table 3.2 Debate viewing (2012) by age groups (%)

Watched	18–34s	35–49s	50–64s	65+
All/most (combined)	**75**	**88**	**85**	**89**
All of the debate	42	41	45	59
Most of the debate	33	47	39	30
Some/little (combined)	**25**	**11**	**15**	**11**
Some of the debate	21	7	12	10
Little of the debate	4	4	3	1

The basic problem is that these debates have failed to keep pace with the ever-changing world of electronic communication. In an attempt to increase audiences for the debates, two changes should be made. First, the time should be shortened from 90 to 60 minutes. Second, they should be carried on a free live feed on the internet. There is every reason to believe that these two changes alone would significantly increase the audience for these debates.

The on-site audiences

Whereas the vast majority see the debates on television, a favoured few have been able to watch them as part of the on-site audiences. But with the exception of the so-called Town Hall debates, audience members are instructed beforehand 'not to applaud or participate by any means other than silent observation'. That being the case, it is hard to see why they are there at all. Adding weight to the argument for removing them altogether is the fact that they rarely obey these simple instructions. Furthermore, their cheering, jeering and laughter can change the way a particular moment in a debate is perceived by the television audience and can distract attention from the substance of what is being said by the candidates.

Indeed, one could go further. There have been occasions when the audience's audible reaction has played a significant part in the debate. Two examples stand out: the audience reaction to President Reagan's answer to a question about his age in the second debate in 1984, and the audience response to the exchange between Senators Dan Quayle and Lloyd Bentsen over any comparison of the former with President John F. Kennedy in the vice presidential debate in 1988. On-site audiences also add to the cost of staging the debates by necessitating a large auditorium. It would be much better to dispense altogether with the on-site audience except for any Town Hall style debates.

The timing

The timing of the debates is critical. The most important issue here is how near to Election Day the final presidential debate is held. In 2012 the third and final debate between President Obama and Governor Romney was held just 15 days before Election Day. As Table 3.3 shows, this is almost a week nearer to Election Day than in the previous four election cycles. Indeed, in only two cycles — 1976 and 1980 — had the final debate been held nearer to Election Day.

Table 3.3 Number of days between the last presidential debate and Election Day, 1960–2016

Year	Days between last debate and Election Day	Year	Days between last debate and Election Day
1960	18	1996	20
1976	11	2000	21
1980	7	2004	20
1984	16	2008	20
1988	26	2012	15
1992	15	2016	20

There are two important issues here. First, conventional wisdom has it that the nearer the final debate is held to Election Day, the more potentially significant the debate can be in affecting the election outcome. In 1980, the only debate between President Carter and Governor Reagan was held on 28 October, just a week before Election Day. Writing 25 years later, Andrew Busch (*Reagan's Victory: The Presidential Election of 1980 and the Rise of the Right*, University Press of Kansas, 2005) stated that 'the debate may have been the critical turning point in the campaign'. In the days that followed the debate, polls that had been neck and neck showed Reagan with a significant lead. On 4 November, Reagan won 44 states. Seeing how decisive a late debate could be, never again would candidates — incumbents or challengers — agree to a debate so late in the campaign. It was just too risky.

But the second issue concerns the recent rise in early voting. As of January 2015, 33 states plus the District of Columbia permitted early voting. With so many states now offering early voting, the proportion of those who cast their ballots before Election Day has increased significantly in recent elections. In 1992, only 7% of ballots were cast before Election Day but by 2012 this figure had risen to 32% (see Figure 3.2).

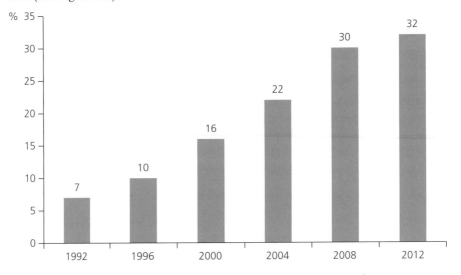

Figure 3.2 Percentage of ballots cast by early voters in presidential elections, 1992–2012

In the light of this development, it seems absurd to hold a TV debate just 15 days before Election Day, as occurred in 2012. It was estimated that in eight battleground states in 2012, almost 7% of those who would vote had already cast their ballots by the time of the final Obama–Romney debate. Indeed, almost 4% of votes had already been cast in these states even before the second debate. It would therefore be good if the schedule of debates were moved to earlier in the campaign. This is indeed what will occur in 2016 with the final debate scheduled 20 days before Election Day.

The participants

In only two elections have candidates other than Democrats and Republicans participated in the televised debates. In 1980, the first debate was between Republican challenger Ronald Reagan and independent candidate John Anderson. President Carter refused to make it a threesome. Twelve years later, the 1992 debates included independent candidate Ross Perot and his running-mate James Stockdale. But Perot was not invited to participate in the debates in 1996 — an election in which he received more than 8 million votes.

The Commission on Presidential Debates (CPD) administers a two-part test to decide whether or not a third party or independent candidate will be invited to participate in the presidential debates (see Box 3.1). But since that test was established more than two decades ago, the proportion of the American electorate who see themselves as 'independent' or 'non-aligned' has increased significantly. In March 2014, a Pew Research poll found that 50% of 18–33-year-olds — the so-called millennial generation — saw themselves as political independents.

Box 3.1   Criteria for inclusion of third party and independent candidates in presidential debates

- Any candidate included must have the ability to be elected in the general election by qualifying for ballot inclusion in states adding up to at least 270 electoral votes.
- Any such candidate must also reach at least 15% in independent national polls in the period leading up to the debates.

The CPD ruling is something of a self-fulfilling prophecy. By being denied a place in the televised debates, candidates (such as Green Party candidate Ralph Nader in 2000) are denied an opportunity to gain a hearing that might push their support towards the 15% threshold. One meritorious reform that has been suggested is that the threshold should be lowered to 10% for the first debate, remain at 15% for the second, and be raised to 25% for the third. This would have the advantage of facilitating participation by other candidates early in the campaign, giving them a chance to grow their support. But if they failed to do so, they would then be excluded at later stages.

The post-debate spin

Immediately after each debate, the media's focus immediately switches to 'spin alley', where representatives of each candidate try to convince the media that their candidate won the debate. In the days when TV was just about the sole medium of instant communication, this spectacle might have had some purpose. But in today's world of Twitter and texting it seems merely a tired and tedious routine, where the self-selected elite of the media try to make themselves and the post-debate spinning almost as important as the debate itself. The whole thing should be consigned to the dustbin.

Conclusions

The televised presidential debates are undoubtedly an important part of the election campaign. Each debate, and especially the first one, remains a potential turning point in the campaign. It offers a chance for front-runners to stumble and for those lagging behind to improve their standing in the polls. But for all their strengths they continue to be more about style than substance. What we tend to remember about them are a haggard and sweaty face (Nixon 1960), a misstatement (Ford 1976), a good joke (Reagan 1984) and a candidate caught looking at his watch (Bush 1992). Few can recall any memorable moment of substantive debate.

And finally, there's that word — 'debate'. For in their five decades of existence they have never really been debates at all — more like joint press conferences. The one thing that turns off most potential viewers is the lack of conversation and interaction between the candidates themselves. It's all so stilted and somewhat predictable. The roundtable format — first used for a presidential debate in the second debate in 2000, and used for the final debate in both 2008 and 2012 — may be the format most likely to engender genuine discussion. But we also need debates to be more fluid, less tied up with intricate time limits. We need moderators who are more relaxed and who, like a good sports umpire, are not themselves the centre of attention. But we also need eloquent and confident candidates who genuinely want to engage with each other and the electorate. Maybe that's asking way too much.

Questions

1 When did televised presidential debates begin?
2 How has electronic communication changed since then?
3 What concerns do the data in Table 3.2 and Figure 3.1 give us concerning the TV audiences for these debates?
4 What problems can be created by the on-site audience during a debate?
5 Why does the author think the debates should be held earlier in the campaign?
6 What criteria do third party and independent candidates have to satisfy in order to be included in the debates?
7 In each section of this chapter, the author suggests possible reforms that might improve the debates. List each of these proposed reforms and say why each might improve the debates.

Chapter 4

What's the Supreme Court been deciding in 2015?

What you need to know

- The Supreme Court is the highest federal court in the USA.
- The Court is made up of nine justices, appointed by the president, for life.
- Of the current nine justices, five were appointed by Republican presidents and four by Democrats.
- The Supreme Court has the power of judicial review. This is the power to declare acts of Congress or actions of the executive branch — or acts or actions of state governments — unconstitutional, and thereby null and void.
- By this power of judicial review, the Court acts as the umpire of the Constitution and plays a leading role in safeguarding Americans' rights and liberties.

This chapter updates material on the Supreme Court on pages 314–31 of the textbook (Anthony J. Bennett, *A2 US Government and Politics*, 4th edition, 2013).

The Supreme Court's term that ended in June 2015 will probably be remembered for two landmark decisions — one on same-sex marriage and another on President Obama's healthcare reforms. The President will feel well pleased with both. Given that the Court is made up predominantly of Republican-appointed justices, and that the Court is thought to have a natural conservative majority — even if not an always clearly defined one — this is in itself a considerable surprise. In this chapter we shall consider these two landmark decisions, as well as three decisions dealing with First Amendment rights, and one concerning the administration of the death penalty. In Chapter 5, we shall analyse the Court's most recent term as a whole.

First Amendment rights

Anthony Elonis, a native of Pennsylvania, claimed he was 'just an aspiring rapper' who liked to post violent lyrics on Facebook. But after he had made numerous postings threatening various individuals — including his estranged wife, his boss and an FBI agent — with murder, a federal jury found him guilty of transmitting 'communications containing threats to injure another person' and he was sentenced to nearly four years in prison. In *Elonis* v *United States* the Supreme Court was being asked to decide whether these Facebook postings constituted a genuine threat of violence, or whether they counted as constitutionally protected

Table 4.1 Significant Supreme Court decisions, 2014–15 term

Case	Concerning	Decision
Elonis v *United States*	Freedom of speech on social media	8–1
Walker v *Texas Division, Sons of Confederate Veterans*	Confederate flag symbols on vehicle licence plates	5–4
Williams-Yulee v *Florida Bar*	Fundraising in state judicial elections	5–4
Glossip v *Gross*	Lethal injection as a means of administering the death penalty	5–4
Obergefell v *Hodges*	Power of state legislatures to prohibit same-sex marriage	5–4
King v *Burwell*	Allowance of tax credits to people who bought health insurance through the federal government	6–3

speech under the First Amendment. It was a good example of words written in the eighteenth century (the First Amendment) being applied to society in the twenty-first century.

In an 8–1 decision, the Court decided for Mr Elonis, thereby making it harder to prosecute people for apparent threats made on social media. Writing for the majority, Chief Justice Roberts said that prosecutors must do more than prove that reasonable people would view the statements as threats. They had to prove some kind of clear intent to carry out the threats. However, the Court failed to offer any specificity as to what 'clear intent' might look like. Justice Thomas was the lone dissenter in this case, stating that he would have upheld Elonis's conviction and that the vagueness of the basis upon which the majority had made its decision 'throws everyone from judges to Facebook users into a state of uncertainty'.

The Court's decision in another First Amendment case would perhaps have passed largely unnoticed but for the context in which it was announced. On the evening of 17 June 2015, nine members of an African American church in Charleston, South Carolina, were shot dead by a 21-year-old white man, Dylann Roof. Roof was pictured on a white supremacist website posing with the Confederate flag and various pieces of racist propaganda. The shootings sparked a national debate about the appropriateness or otherwise of the public display of the Confederate flag in twenty-first-century America.

The very next day, the Supreme Court announced its decision in *Walker* v *Texas Division, Sons of Confederate Veterans*. First, a quick bit of background. In the United States, all motorised road vehicles carry a licence plate issued by the state in which the vehicle is licensed. These plates often carry a state slogan such as 'Arizona: Grand Canyon State', 'California: The Golden State' or 'New York: The Empire State'. Some states include advertisements such as 'Louisiana: Sportsman's Paradise'. Others include state flags or symbols.

Table 4.2 The ideological line-up of the Supreme Court, 2014–15

Liberal quartet	Swing justice	Conservative quartet
Ruth Bader Ginsburg	Anthony Kennedy	John Roberts
Sonia Sotomayor		Antonin Scalia
Stephen Breyer		Clarence Thomas
Elena Kagan		Samuel Alito

In this 5–4 decision, the Court allowed the state of Texas to reject specialty car licence plates bearing the Confederate flag. The make-up of the majority was especially noteworthy, consisting as it did of the Court's liberal quartet (see Table 4.2) joined by Justice Clarence Thomas, the noted conservative and the only African American on the Court. The Court's decision was immediately taken up by three state governors — Terry McAuliffe of Virginia, Pat McCrory of North Carolina and Larry Hogan of Maryland — all of whom announced plans to stop such licence plates being issued in their states. In his dissenting opinion, Justice Samuel Alito wrote in a way that encapsulated the public debate following the Charleston church shootings:

> The Confederate flag is a controversial symbol. To the Texas Sons of Confederate Veterans it is said to evoke the memory of their ancestors and the soldiers who fought for the South in the Civil War. To others it symbolises slavery, segregation and hatred.

What the Court decided in this case was that because vehicle license plates are issued by the state governments, those governments can decide what messages they carry. In the words of Justice Breyer, the states can use their licence plates to 'urge action, promote tourism, and to tout local industries'. But they do not have to match those messages they prefer with messages or symbols that they oppose.

In another freedom of speech ruling, *Williams-Yulee v Florida Bar*, the Court ruled that states may prohibit candidates in state judicial elections from personally asking their supporters for campaign contributions. Judges in the 39 states that hold judicial elections raise money from lawyers who appear before them, though usually this is done through campaign committees rather than by personal requests for money. Indeed in 30 states, personal solicitation of money is banned. Lanell Williams-Yulee was reprimanded and ordered to pay $1,860 in costs after signing a fund-raising letter when she ran for a county court judgeship in Florida. Florida is one of those states that ban direct fund-raising in judicial elections. The Florida Supreme Court had upheld the ban and the penalty imposed, saying that it helped 'to ensure that judges engaged in campaign activities are able to maintain their status as fair and impartial arbiters of the law'. Williams-Yulee had claimed that the ban limited her First Amendment rights of freedom of speech. But the Supreme Court disagreed.

The case was decided by a 5–4 majority with another unusual grouping; this time it was Chief Justice John Roberts who joined the Court's liberal quartet to form the five-member majority. 'A state's decision to elect judges does not compel it to compromise public confidence in their integrity,' stated Roberts. 'Judges are not politicians,' he added, 'even when they come to the bench by way of the ballot.' Addressing the First Amendment issues, Roberts wrote:

> Speech about public issues and the qualifications of candidates for elected office commands the highest level of First Amendment protection. This is one of the rare cases in which a speech restriction stands the strictest scrutiny. Judges charged with exercising strict neutrality and independence cannot supplicate campaign donors without diminishing public confidence in judicial integrity.

In his dissenting opinion, Justice Antonin Scalia wrote that the decision was merely a disguised attack on judicial elections 'that flattens one settled First Amendment principle after another'. Justice Anthony Kennedy, another dissenter, claimed that the Court had censured Ms Williams-Yulee's speech, adding that 'whether an election is the best way to choose a judge is itself the subject of fair debate, but once the people of a state choose to have elections, the First Amendment protects the candidate's right to speak'.

Eighth Amendment

The Supreme Court has made a number of rulings recently on the Eighth Amendment's prohibition of 'cruel and unusual punishments' (see Table 4.3). In 2015, the Court revisited an area upon which it last ruled in 2008 as to whether lethal injection — the method used by most of the states who impose the death penalty — contravened the Eighth Amendment.

Table 4.3 Recent decisions concerning the Eighth Amendment

Case	Decision
Ring v *Arizona* (2002)	Death sentences must be imposed by juries, not judges
Atkins v *Virginia* (2002)	No execution of mentally retarded criminals
Roper v *Simmons* (2004)	No execution for crimes committed by under-18s
Baze v *Rees* (2008)	Lethal injection does not violate the Eighth Amendment
Hall v *Florida* (2014)	States may not have a fixed numerical score to determine mental retardation in death penalty decisions

First, some background. Currently 19 of the 50 states, plus the District of Columbia, do not use the death penalty. These are almost all in the northern tier of states, plus the North-east, the Mid-Atlantic, as well as Alaska and Hawaii. Six states have abolished the death penalty in the last ten years — New Jersey (2007), New Mexico (2009), Illinois (2011), Connecticut (2012), Maryland (2013) and Nebraska (2015). At the other end of the scale, five states dominate the death penalty league table with Texas clearly in the lead (see Table 4.4). Of the 1,413 people executed in the United States since the death penalty was reinstated in

1976, 1,238 (88%) have been by lethal injection. This is why the Court's decisions about lethal injection are so important. If the Court were to declare this form of execution unconstitutional, it could be the death knell for the death penalty in the United States.

In *Glossip* v *Gross* (2015) the Court again ruled, however, that lethal injection does not violate the Eighth Amendment. The 5–4 decision found the conservative quartet of John Roberts, Antonin Scalia, Clarence Thomas and Samuel Alito joined by Anthony Kennedy in the majority, with the liberal foursome in the minority. Of the six decisions we are considering, this was the only one to have the liberals on the losing side. Justice Scalia accused the minority of wanting to end the death penalty through undemocratic means — in other words, by a decision of the Court. Scalia argued that the matter should be decided only by the people, just as the constitutional framers intended. This, claimed Scalia, is a decision for the people and their elected representatives, not for judges.

Table 4.4 Executions since 1976 and numbers currently on death row (selected states)

State	Executions since 1976	Number currently on death row*
Texas	528	261
Oklahoma	112	49
Virginia	110	8
Florida	90	395
Missouri	84	31

*As at August 2015

Same-sex marriage

If you're someone in America who supports gay rights then Justice Anthony Kennedy is your man. If you're someone in America who opposes gay rights then Justice Antonin Scalia is your man. Two justices, appointed by the same president — Ronald Reagan — within less than 18 months of each other, who have served together on the same court for more than a quarter of a century, who often vote together on important decisions, who share the same religious faith — both are Roman Catholics — and who even live on the same northern Virginia street, epitomise the two ends of the spectrum when it comes to this most contentious of issues. Kennedy has written all of the Supreme Court's most important gay rights decisions: protecting the civil rights of homosexuals in *Romer* v *Evans* (1996); abolishing anti-sodomy laws in *Lawrence* v *Texas* (2003); and ruling in *United States* v *Windsor* (2013) that the federal government must recognise same-sex marriages.

In 2015, the Court reached yet another stepping-stone on the gay rights path — whether or not state legislatures have the power to prohibit same-sex marriages, and whether such state bans violate the Fourteenth Amendment, which

forbids the states from denying the equal protection of the laws to any person within their jurisdictions. The case was *Obergefell* v *Hodges*. It was brought by James Obergefell, who had married John Arthur in Maryland in 2013. But their state of residence, Ohio, would not recognise the marriage. Arthur was terminally ill, and when Obergefell asked to be named as the surviving spouse on the death certificate, the state authorities refused. Obergefell then filed in the federal court, claiming an infringement of his Fourteenth Amendment rights by the Ohio ban on same-sex marriage. The trial court (July 2013) found in Obergefell's favour, but the appeals court (November 2014) overturned that decision, stating that the ban was not unconstitutional and no rights had been infringed. The argument reached the Supreme Court in April 2015 and the Court announced its decision on 26 June 2015. This was by far and away the landmark decision of the term.

Box 4.1 **Justice Anthony Kennedy, majority opinion,
Obergefell v *Hodges* (2015)**

No union is more profound than marriage, for it embodies the highest ideals of love, fidelity, devotion, sacrifice and family. In forming a marital union, two people become something greater than once they were. As some of the petitioners in these cases demonstrate, marriage embodies a love that may endure even past death. It would misunderstand these men and women to say they disrespect the idea of marriage. Their plea is that they do respect it, respect it so deeply that they seek to find its fulfilment for themselves. Their hope is not to be condemned to live in loneliness, excluded from one of civilisation's oldest institutions. They ask for equal dignity in the eyes of the law. The Constitution grants them that right.

Here was yet another 5–4 decision with Justice Kennedy writing for the liberal majority. Kennedy resorted to the soaring oratory he had used in previous decisions on the same subject (see Box 4.1). The 'in' word was 'dignity', which appeared nine times in his majority opinion. But quite where he found it in the Constitution is slightly baffling. The Fourteenth Amendment mentions only 'life, liberty, or property'. But according to Kennedy, in addition these liberties 'extend to certain personal choices central to individual dignity and autonomy, including intimate choices that define personal identity and beliefs'. It sounded a bit like *Roe* v *Wade* reborn.

In the view of the dissenting minority, this was an issue that should have been left up to individual states to decide. 'This Supreme Court is not a legislature,' wrote Chief Justice Roberts. 'Whether same-sex marriage is a good idea should be of no concern to us. Under the Constitution, judges have power to say what the law is, not what it should be. The people who ratified the Constitution authorised the courts to exercise "neither force nor will but merely judgement"' — a quotation from Alexander Hamilton. It's a classic statement from a strict constructionist (see below).

US Government & Politics

Strict constructionist

A justice of the Supreme Court who interprets the Constitution in a strict, literal or conservative fashion, and who tends to stress the retention of as much power as possible by the governments of the individual states.

Justice Scalia lampooned Kennedy's tendency to write in what Robert Barnes in the *Washington Post* described as 'a lofty, writing-for-history tone'. Wrote Scalia: 'The opinion is couched in a style that is as pretentious as its content is egotistic', adding for good measure that 'the opinion's showy profundities are often profoundly incoherent'. Scalia was equally scathing of the majority's finding the right to marriage in the Constitution. 'They have discovered in the Fourteenth Amendment,' commented Scalia, 'a "fundamental right" overlooked by every person alive at the time of [the Constitution's] ratification, and almost everyone else in the time since.' He then added sarcastically:

> Those justices know that limiting marriage to one man and one woman is contrary to reason; they know that an institution as old as government itself, and accepted by every nation in history until 15 years ago, cannot possibly be supported by anything other than ignorance and bigotry.

Justice Alito in his dissent worried that those who fail to accept the new view of marriage will be in for a hard time, fearing that this decision 'will be used to vilify Americans who are unwilling to assent to the new orthodoxy'. Some will think that Alito was soon proved right by the imprisonment of Kentucky county clerk Kim Davis when she refused to issue a marriage licence to a gay couple because it went against her religious beliefs.

Box 4.2 Chief Justice John Roberts, minority opinion, *Obergefell* v *Hodges* (2015)

The majority's decision is an act of will, not legal judgement. The right it announces has no basis in the Constitution or this Court's precedent. The majority expressly disclaims judicial 'caution' and omits even a pretence of humility, openly relying on its desire to remake society according to its own 'new insight' into the 'nature of injustice'. As a result, the Court invalidates the marriage laws of more than half the States and orders the transformation of a social institution that has formed the basis of human society for millennia, for the Kalahari Bushmen and the Han Chinese, the Carthaginians and the Aztecs. Just who do we think we are?

President Obama was, however, effusive in his praise of the Court's decision. In a statement issued soon afterwards, Obama hailed it as 'a victory for America' and one that 'made our Union a little more perfect'. Was this the same Barack Obama who as recently as August 2008 told southern California mega-church pastor Rick Warren that his definition of marriage was 'the union between a man and a woman', adding that 'for me as a Christian, it is also a sacred union [because]

God's in the mix'? Perhaps he thinks that Justice Kennedy has now replaced the Almighty as the arbiter on matters of marriage. Whatever the case, it is startling that this view, held and openly spoken about by the President just seven years earlier, had now been declared illegal as a basis for law in all 50 states.

'Obamacare' again

The facts behind the case known as *King* v *Burwell* are slightly complicated. One of the main aims of the 2010 Affordable Care Act (a.k.a. Obamacare) was to provide health insurance to as many Americans as possible. States were encouraged to set up exchanges, or marketplaces, where individuals could buy health insurance, and there would be subsidies from the federal government for people who needed them. The Act also made provision for people who lived in a state that did not set up an exchange to buy their health insurance through exchanges set up by the federal government.

A section in the law stated that subsidies would be available through the Internal Revenue Service (IRS) to anyone who bought insurance through an exchange 'established by the state'. The question arose as to whether that phrase applied only to exchanges established by the states, or to the federal government exchanges as well. The IRS had understood the provision to include the federal exchanges. This was important because, in 34 states, the federal exchanges were the only option. But this legal challenge claimed that the IRS had exceeded the authority Congress had given it by offering federally funded tax credits to those who had bought through the federal government's exchanges.

In a 6–3 decision, the Supreme Court upheld the IRS's action as consistent with the intention of the Affordable Care Act, thus saving Obamacare. 'Congress passed the Affordable Care Act to improve health insurance markets, not destroy them,' Chief Justice Roberts wrote on behalf of the majority. Had the decision gone the other way, around 6 million lower-income Americans living in the states where the federal health exchange was the only option would have lost their federal subsidies to help them buy their health insurance. This would have created havoc and probably wrecked the law. Indeed, that was probably the undeclared aim and wish of the plaintiffs in this case.

The phrase in question was clearly an example of poorly crafted legislation. But six justices were prepared to help Congress out and keep the law intact. The three dissenting justices — Antonin Scalia, Clarence Thomas and Samuel Alito — were critical of this tactic. 'The Court's decision reflects the philosophy that judges should endure whatever interpretive distortions it takes in order to correct a supposed flaw in the statute,' wrote Scalia. 'It is up to Congress to design laws with care,' he added, 'and it is up to the people to hold them to account if they fail to carry out that responsibility.' Scalia described the majority's reasoning as 'quite absurd' and 'interpretive jiggery-pokery'.

This is the second time in three years that Chief Justice Roberts has come to the Act's rescue by siding with the Court's liberal quartet. He did so first in *National*

Federation of Independent Business v *Sebelius* in 2012, much to the anger of political conservatives. Their reaction was much the same this time around. One wag suggested that the law should henceforth be referred to as 'Roberts-care', given that the chief justice had done more than most to secure its future.

Conclusions

The Court certainly made some high-profile rulings during this term, the one concerning same-sex marriage being by far the most notable. Had the Obamacare decision gone the other way, that would also have been just as significant. As we shall see more clearly in the next chapter, the Court took a much more liberal path during this term than it had done for many a year. Indeed, five of the six significant decisions we have considered here were decided with the liberal quartet in the majority. Quite a record. And Table 4.5 shows how much more frequently the liberal quartet were in the majority on this term's significant decisions than were the conservatives. Now read on in Chapter 5 for a detailed analysis of the Court's term as a whole and see how this term compared with recent ones.

Table 4.5 Justices in the majority in significant decisions, 2014–15 term

	Elonis	*Walker*	*Williams-Yulee*	*Glossip*	*Obergefell*	*King*
Roberts	✓		✓	✓		✓
Scalia	✓			✓		
Kennedy	✓			✓	✓	✓
Thomas		✓		✓		
Ginsburg	✓	✓	✓		✓	✓
Breyer	✓	✓	✓		✓	✓
Alito	✓			✓		
Sotomayor	✓	✓	✓		✓	✓
Kagan	✓	✓	✓		✓	✓

Questions

1 Why did the Court find in favour of Anthony Elonis in the case of *Elonis* v *United States*?
2 Why was the *Walker* v *Texas* decision so topical? What did it say?
3 Why did the Court find against Ms Williams-Yulee in the case concerning money raising in state judicial elections?
4 What was the significance of the *Glossip* v *Gross* decision for the future use of the death penalty in America?
5 Summarise both the majority and minority opinions in the same-sex marriage decision.
6 How did Chief Justice Roberts again come to the aid of Obamacare?

Chapter 5

The Supreme Court: the 2014–15 term

This chapter updates the material on the Supreme Court in Chapter 7 of the textbook (Anthony J. Bennett, *A2 US Government and Politics*, 4th edition, 2013).

In Chapter 4 we analysed six significant decisions handed down by the Supreme Court in its term which began in October 2014 and ended in June 2015. But these were only six of the 75 decisions handed down by the Court during this term. As Table 5.1 shows, that figure of 75 decisions is roughly in line with the figures for the last four terms, but represents a significant decrease on the 86 decisions handed down in the 2009–10 term. It was a stated aim of John Roberts when he joined the Court as chief justice in 2005 that he wanted to prune the number of decisions made each term by the Court. Of these 75 cases, 67 (89%) originated from the United States Courts of Appeal and just five (7%) from the state courts. Of the remaining three cases, two came from the court for the District of Columbia and the other was a case of original jurisdiction.

Unity and division

Having hit a record high of 65% in the previous term, the number of unanimous decisions fell back in this term to the lowest for six years, since the 2008–09 term that saw just 36% of unanimous decisions. Unsurprisingly, a fall in unanimity was matched by a rise in 5–4 decisions, up from 14% to 26%. Roberts had been proud of the Court's degree of agreement in the previous term, though some thought it was all rather artificial, as we discussed in last year's *Update*.

Table 5.1 Total, unanimous and 5–4 decisions, 2009–15

Term	2009–10	2010–11	2011–12	2012–13	2013–14	2014–15
Number of decisions	86	80	75	78	72	**75**
% which were unanimous	46%	48%	44%	49%	65%	**40%**
% which were 5–4 decisions	19%	20%	20%	29%	14%	**26%**

The 5–4 decisions

The most noteworthy fact of the Court's most recent term was the extent to which the liberal wing of the Court won the day on so many of the 5–4 decisions. Of the 19 5–4 decisions, the liberal quartet plus Justice Kennedy were in the majority in 8 (42%) of them, whilst the conservative quartet plus Kennedy were in the majority in only 5 (26%). That was the lowest score for the conservatives since Roberts and Alito joined the Court ten years ago (see Table 5.2). This trend also shows itself in the frequency with which the justices were in the majority on these 5–4 decisions. Whereas liberal Stephen Breyer was in the majority in 14 (74%) of the 5–4 decisions, conservative Antonin Scalia was in the majority in only 6 (32%), with fellow conservatives Thomas and Alito doing little better (see Table 5.3).

Table 5.2 Percentage of conservative victories in 5–4 decisions

Term	Percentage of conservative victories in 5–4 decisions
2005–06	45
2006–07	54
2007–08	33
2008–09	48
2009–10	50
2010–11	63
2011–12	33
2012–13	43
2013–14	40
2014–15	**26**

Table 5.3 Frequency of justices in the majority in 5–4 decisions, 2014–15

Justice	Frequency in majority in 5-4 decisions
Stephen Breyer	14
Anthony Kennedy	14
Sonia Sotomayor	13
Ruth Bader Ginsburg	12
Elena Kagan	10
John Roberts	10
Samuel Alito	9
Clarence Thomas	7
Antonin Scalia	6

What was the reason for this liberal revival? According to the noted Supreme Court watcher Adam Liptak, writing in the *New York Times*, it was 'the product of discipline on the left side of the Court and disarray on the right'. As a result, the 2014–15 term was the most liberal since the late 1960s, according to two political science measurements of Court voting data. Eric Posner, law professor at the University of Chicago, agreed: 'The most interesting thing about this term is the acceleration of a long-term trend of disagreement among the Republican-appointed judges, while the Democratic-appointed judges continue to march in lock step.' We shall return to this particular point later on.

So why are the liberal justices so much more disciplined? Many analysts credit the leadership of Ruth Bader Ginsburg, the senior member of the liberal justices, with now 22 years' service on the Court. In a recent interview, Justice Ginsburg admitted that 'we have made a concerted effort to speak with one voice in important cases'.

And why are the conservatives so splintered? There are probably two reasons. First, it is probably true to say that Scalia, Thomas and Alito are more individualistic — or should that be idiosyncratic — than Breyer, Ginsburg, Sotomayor and Kagan. They are more prone to act like prima donnas. Second, as conservative litigators have tried to move the law more to the right, they have been bringing cases to the Supreme Court that both Anthony Kennedy and John Roberts think are unreasonable. This year's Obamacare case is a good example, and the result was that both Roberts and Kennedy joined the Court's liberals in rejecting the challenge to health insurance subsidies provided through federal exchanges. Only Scalia, Thomas and Alito were prepared to support it.

Identical twins and odd couples

This theme of liberal discipline and conservative splintering can be seen in Table 5.4, where we consider who were the two justices most often in agreement. Whereas in the previous term the identical twins were two conservatives — Clarence Thomas and Samuel Alito — this term it was the two liberal Clinton appointees, Ruth Bader Ginsburg and Stephen Breyer. They agreed in 94% of the cases. Furthermore, Ginsburg agreed with Kagan in 93% of cases and with Sotomayor in 92%. Not so much identical twins as identical quads. By contrast, Roberts's highest level of agreement was with Scalia at just 84%, whilst Thomas's highest level was with Alito at 81%.

Table 5.4 Agreement and disagreement between justices, 2009–15

Term	2009–10	2010–11	2011–12	2012–13	2013–14	2014–15
Two justices most in agreement	Ginsburg Sotomayor	Roberts Alito	Scalia Thomas	Ginsburg Kagan	Thomas Alito	Breyer Ginsburg
Two justices most in disagreement	Thomas Stevens	Alito Ginsburg	Scalia Ginsburg	Alito Ginsburg	Alito Sotomayor	Thomas Sotomayor

The two justices most in disagreement this term were Thomas and Sotomayor, who disagreed on 50% of all cases and on 84% of non-unanimous cases. This confirms what we were beginning to see in the previous term: that Obama appointee Sotomayor is beginning to prove the most reliably liberal vote on the Court.

Differences in time and approach

Some justices work quicker than others, as Table 5.5 shows. Whereas Justice Scalia took an average of only 81 days from oral argument to announcing his majority opinions, the ponderous Justice Kennedy took 120 days, well over the

95-day average. This is even more remarkable when one adds into the mix that Scalia authored more majority opinions (nine) than any other justice, whilst Kennedy authored the least (six).

Table 5.5 Days between oral argument and majority opinion

Majority opinion author	Days
Scalia	81
Sotomayor	85
Ginsburg	88
Thomas	88
Roberts	90
Breyer	94
Kagan	104
Alito	109
Kennedy	120
Average	**95 days**

The justices also differ in the way they operate at the oral argument stage. Of course, one always has to begin such a discussion by drawing attention to Justice Thomas's perpetual silence in the courtroom. He has failed to ask a question at oral argument now for 10 years. Justice Scalia again held the record for asking the most questions at oral argument (see Table 5.6). Indeed, he even raised the bar from an average of 19 in the 2013–14 term to 22 in this term. The other justices continued a frequency of questioning similar to that in the previous term. It illustrates the different *modus operandi* of the justices.

Table 5.6 Average number of questions per oral argument

Justice	Average
Scalia	22.0
Sotomayor	19.0
Breyer	17.5
Roberts	13.8
Kagan	12.7
Ginsburg	11.1
Kennedy	10.1
Alito	9.4
Thomas	0.0

Justice Ginsburg may not ask very many questions, but Table 5.7 (page 46) shows that she was once again the quickest off the mark during this term, asking the first question in almost one-third of cases. As one of the more senior justices on the Court these days, that seems perfectly allowable. What colleagues think of Justice Sotomayor's frequent early interruptions, one is not too sure. The somewhat laconic Stephen Breyer was never the first questioner in this term's oral arguments.

Table 5.7 Frequency as the first questioner at oral argument

Justice	Frequency (%)
Ginsburg	29
Sotomayor	21
Scalia	18
Kennedy	16
Roberts	7
Kagan	6
Alito	3
Breyer	0
Thomas	0

So whose Court is it anyway?

So who is the leading justice of today's Supreme Court? We have already suggested that Justice Ginsburg has been a most influential voice in the Court during 2014–15. Her leadership of the liberal wing of the Court, as well as her ability to appeal to swing justice Anthony Kennedy to create a five-member majority, have been important ingredients in making this such a good year for the liberals.

Table 5.8 Justice(s) most in the majority, 2009–15

Term	2009–10	2010–11	2011–12	2012–13	2013–14	2014–15
Justice(s) most in the majority in all decisions	Kennedy Roberts	Kennedy	Kennedy	Kennedy	Kennedy	Breyer
Justice(s) most in majority in 5–4 decisions	Kennedy Thomas Scalia	Kennedy	Kennedy	Kennedy	Kennedy	Kennedy Breyer

But one could also make out a case for Stephen Breyer being regarded as the Court's leading justice. After all, as Table 5.8 shows, he was the justice most frequently in the majority during this term. He was in the majority in 92% of all decisions and in 86% of all divided decisions.

Equally, one could make out a case — as we often have done in previous years — that Justice Kennedy is the most influential person on the Court. In 5–4 decisions, Justice Kennedy has been the justice most frequently in the majority (either solely or jointly) for the past 11 terms, a quite extraordinary record, and as Table 5.8 shows, in four of the past five years he has held that record on his own. In this term, Kennedy also played his role in moving the Court to the left. Of the 19 5–4 decisions, 13 split along the usual ideological lines with the liberal quartet on one side and the conservative quartet on the other. But this term, Kennedy sided with the liberals in 8 and with the conservatives in only 5. In previous terms, Kennedy had leant to the right about two-thirds of the time.

And what about the Chief?

But of course, as we know, the traditional way of identifying the Court is to name it for the Chief Justice — hence we have most recently had the Warren Court (Earl Warren, 1953–69), the Burger Court (Warren Burger, 1969–86) and the Rehnquist Court (1986–2005). So how do you view John Roberts? Is the Court *his* court?

It may be the case that Roberts is too much of a pragmatist to be a strong influence on the Court. He's not really an ideologue. It's as he told the Senate Judiciary Committee during his confirmation hearings back in 2005: 'I have no platform.' To Roberts, 'justices are servants of the law', they are 'like umpires' and 'umpires don't make the rules, they apply them'. Just consider Roberts's positions on two landmark decisions on two consecutive days during the final week of this past term. As Adam Liptak remarked in the *New York Times* ('Angering Conservatives and Liberals, Chief Justice Roberts Defends Steady Restraint', 26 June 2015), on the Thursday when Roberts voted with the liberals and helped save the Affordable Care Act for a second time, conservatives accused him of everything short of treason, whilst on the Friday when he dissented from a decision establishing a constitutional right to same-sex marriage, liberals said that he had 'tarnished his legacy and landed on the wrong side of history'.

Box 5.1	Extracts from two opinions by Chief Justice Roberts

In a democracy the power to make the law rests with those chosen by the people.

King v *Burwell* (2015)

It can be tempting for judges to confuse their own preferences with the requirements of the law. The majority today neglects that restrained conception of the judicial role. It seizes for itself a question the Constitution leaves to the people.

Obergefell v *Hodges* (2015)

Liptak sees Roberts as trying to cast himself 'as a steady practitioner of judicial modesty', very much in line with how he set out his stall at his confirmation hearings. As Liptak observed, 'he employed very similar language in these two cases to suggest that his votes were consistent and principled' (see Box 5.1). Indeed, to read a Roberts opinion is more akin to reading a political science paper than a judicial judgement, for he often spends quite some time laying out his own judicial principles and how he thinks the Court should operate, and how it is distinct from a legislative body (see Box 5.2). Roberts claimed in his *Obergefell* dissent that the majority's argument was that the Due Process Clause gives same-sex couples a fundamental right to marry 'because it will be good for them and for society'. Added Roberts: 'If I were a legislator, I would certainly consider that view as a matter of social policy. But as a judge, I find the majority's position indefensible as a matter of constitutional law.'

Box 5.2 Extract from opinion by Chief Justice Roberts

Understand well what this dissent is about: It is not about whether, in my judgment, the institution of marriage should be changed to include same-sex couples. It is instead about whether, in our democratic republic, that decision should rest with the people acting through their elected representatives, or with five lawyers who happen to hold commissions authorizing them to resolve legal disputes according to law. The Constitution leaves no doubt about the answer.

Obergefell v *Hodges* (2015)

As we have remarked in this publication in previous years, Roberts clearly worries about the role of the Supreme Court in an America as politically polarised as it is. He well nigh bristles at accusations that the Court's decisions are motivated by partisan politics. He hates the references to 'liberal' groups and 'conservative' groups on the Court. In his dissent on same-sex marriage, the Chief Justice reiterated how this opinion and his Obamacare opinion the previous day were entirely consistent. This is how he summed it up:

> Under the Constitution, judges have the power to say what the law is, not what it should be.

In his *New York Times* piece (27 June 2015), Jeffrey Rosen described how in his opinion Roberts embraces 'a bipartisan vision of judicial restraint based on the idea that the Supreme Court should generally defer to the choices of Congress and the state legislatures'. Roberts has a limited view of the Court's role, regardless of who wins, based on the concept of 'the limited institutional role of the Court in relation to the president, Congress and the states'. According to Rosen, Roberts is therefore best described as the 'Umpire in Chief'.

Questions

1 What do the data in Table 5.1 tell us about the Court's 2014–15 term?
2 What evidence do Tables 5.2 and 5.3 give to support the claim that this was a good term for liberals?
3 What reasons are suggested for a 'liberal revival' in this term?
4 What do Tables 5.5, 5.6 and 5.7 tell us about the different ways the justices work?
5 How much influence did Justice Kennedy have during the 2014–15 term?
6 Summarise the judicial philosophy of Chief Justice Roberts.

Chapter 6

The 2016 presidential election

What you need to know

- Presidential elections are held every four years in the years divisible by 4.
- The period before any voting begins (i.e. the calendar year before the election) is known as the Invisible Primary.
- The presidential election is preceded by primaries and caucuses in which the candidates' popularity — or lack of it — is shown and delegates are selected to go to the parties' national conventions.
- The national party conventions are held during the summer before the election.

This chapter updates material on presidential nominations in Chapter 2 of the textbook (Anthony J. Bennett, *A2 US Government and Politics*, 4th edition, 2013), on pages 43–61.

On Tuesday, 8 November 2016, Americans will go to the polls to elect a president, the whole of the House of Representatives and one-third of the Senate. There will also be elections for numerous state offices — governors, state legislators — as well as various state initiatives and constitutional amendments. In this chapter we focus on the presidential race.

Barring unforeseen circumstances, by 2016 President Obama will be coming to the end of his second term in office and will therefore be ineligible for re-election. Thus both the Democrats and the Republicans will have to choose new candidates. Over the last 60 years, this has occurred only four times — 1960, 1988, 2000 and 2008 — when respectively presidents Dwight Eisenhower, Ronald Reagan, Bill Clinton and George W. Bush came to the end of their second terms. On the first three occasions the race was not all that open as the White House party merely nominated the vice president as its presidential candidate — Richard Nixon (1960), George H. W. Bush (1988) and Al Gore (2000). Only in 2008 did both parties nominate candidates who had never before appeared on a national ticket — Barack Obama (D) and John McCain (R).

The Democrats

The Biden factor

So last year, election-watchers were wondering how open 2016 would be. Or to ask the question another way, would Vice President Joe Biden seek the Democratic Party's presidential nomination for 2016? Biden had already sought to be the

presidential nominee of his party twice before — in 1988 and again in 2008. Both attempts were unmitigated disasters. In 1988, he pulled out three months before the Iowa caucuses after allegations of plagiarism in his campaign speech. In 2008, he finished fifth in the Iowa caucuses and pulled out immediately afterwards. So Biden had yet to make it to the New Hampshire primary in a presidential nomination race — hardly the record of a strong candidate.

Biden was also struggling to come to terms with the sudden death in May 2015 of his 46-year-old son, Beau Biden, from brain cancer. The death understandably shocked the whole Biden family and made making plans for the future — including a possible presidential bid by Joe Biden — all the more complicated and difficult. There was much media speculation, most of it ill-informed.

Then, on 22 October, the Vice President took to the podium in the Rose Garden at the White House, flanked by his wife Jill and President Obama. The will-he/won't-he was finally over. The Vice President spoke.

> As the family and I have worked through the grieving process [following Beau's death], I've said all along that it may very well be that that process, by the time we get through it, closes the window on mounting a realistic campaign for president — that it might close. I have concluded it has closed.

So the Vice President would, after all, not be a candidate for the Democratic nomination for the presidency in 2016. This left the race on the Democratic side seemingly straightforward. Without Biden, the presumptive front-runner Hillary Clinton would face only token opposition in the primaries, and the party would stand a very good chance both of selecting its candidate early in the primary season, and also of arriving at the general election campaign united and in a strong financial position.

Hillary's year?

Having said all that, writing a chapter like this is always something of a hostage to fortune. I still remember during 2007 dismissing talk of Barack Obama being a potential front-runner as 'mere media hype'. Such comments can return to haunt you! Well, all the talk as I write is, of course, about Hillary Clinton — the former first lady, senator and secretary of state. Let's consider her potential strengths and weaknesses.

Clinton's strengths will centre on her experience. First, there is her campaign experience. Having endured the 2008 nomination campaign against Obama, she would enter any future race, one presumes at least, better prepared. Second, there is her political experience. She could now add her four years as secretary of state to her eight years in the Senate. Her critics were always somewhat dubious of her claim that her first lady experience was overly relevant to being president. But in 2008 there were concerns that foreign policy was a weakness and now she could claim to be better prepared to deal with the crises facing America from abroad. Six of the 43 people who have been president had previously served as secretary of state, but as Table 6.1 shows, the most recent was James Buchanan, elected in 1856. Some more recent secretaries of state have harboured presidential ambitions — notably Republicans Alexander Haig and Colin Powell. Others have been talked about as potential presidents — Condoleezza Rice, for example.

Table 6.1 Presidents who had previously served as secretary of state

President	Secretary of State	Presidential term
Thomas Jefferson	1790–93	1801–09
James Madison	1801–09	1809–17
James Monroe	1811–17	1817–25
John Quincy Adams	1817–25	1825–29
Martin Van Buren	1829–31	1837–41
James Buchanan	1845–49	1857–61

A third Clinton strength would be her contacts and personal network — both of friends and of fund-raisers — within the Democratic Party after she and her husband have been at or near the centre of Democratic Party politics for two-and-a-half decades.

But Clinton would also bring certain weaknesses. First, it is by no means certain that she will have learnt from the mistakes of her 2008 campaign. She will again have to overcome perceptions of inevitability — of it being 'my turn'. She will have to prove to be a rather more astute organiser of a national campaign than she was eight years ago. And she will still have to try to keep her wayward and garrulous husband under some semblance of control, something she singularly failed to do during the 2008 primaries.

A second potential weakness is the ever-recurring Clinton fatigue factor. Have folk just had enough of the Clintons? The Democrats are not known for giving past failures a second chance. They have much more of a tendency of giving the nomination to the new and the novel — Jimmy Carter in 1976, Bill Clinton in 1992, and Barack Obama in 2008. A third weakness will be her age — 69 by Election Day, making her the second oldest president in history. A fourth weakness is her woodenness as a speaker. 'Many of her events lack energy and emotion,' commented one Democratic insider during the summer of 2015. Others criticised the roundtable discussion format of which Clinton is fond, describing it as 'stilted and artificial'. The late governor of New York, Mario Cuomo, famously remarked that 'you campaign in poetry but govern in prose'. But Hillary Clinton doesn't even have any poetry for the campaign. She campaigns from the telephone directory.

But whatever experience Hillary Clinton would bring to the table, the most important determinant of her success or failure will be whether she brings to the table what voters will be looking for in 2016. She touted her experience in 2008, but that wasn't what voters were looking for. They wanted change, not experience. Maybe, after what some might feel will have been eight years of naivety and inexperience, Hillary's much-vaunted experience will be what voters in the primaries — and maybe the general election — are looking for. However, the noted political commentator David Brooks, writing in his regular column in the *New York Times*, suggested that what voters would be looking for in 2016 is what he called 'that new car smell' — the smell of distinctive freshness, a candidate new to the road in all their pristine cleanliness. Whatever Hillary Clinton has, it's certainly not the 'new car smell'.

The rest of the field

With the early field so dominated by Hillary Clinton, other notable names have clearly been discouraged from throwing their hats into the ring — candidates such as Governor Andrew Cuomo of New York. Cuomo served as secretary of housing and urban development during Bill Clinton's second term and was first elected governor of the Empire State in 2010. His father, Mario Cuomo, served three terms as the state's governor between 1983 and 1994. Another was Elizabeth Warren, the senior senator from Massachusetts, although still in her first term. In 2012 she defeated Republican Scott Brown, who had won the special election following the death of Senator Edward Kennedy in 2009. Warren has shot to stardom during her short career in public life, especially amongst those on the left who still yearn to see a woman elected to the presidency, yet one without all the baggage of a Clinton. But Warren seemed to decide early on that 2016 was not her year. Indeed, once Biden removed himself from the race, Hillary Clinton could have been said to have won the Invisible Primary simply by discouraging so many other big fish from joining the race. All that was left were the political minnows.

As Table 6.2 shows, only four other candidates announced in this race, and two of those — Jim Webb and Lincoln Chafee — lasted only about four months. Webb had served three years in Republican president Ronald Reagan's administration in the 1980s, and Chafee had served eight years in the US Senate – as a Republican. One wondered whether they had entered the right race. That left O'Malley and Sanders. Martin O'Malley had little or no national profile and by mid-October 2015 was averaging 0.5% in the polling on the Real Clear Politics website. It seemed unlikely that he would make it to the end of the year.

Table 6.2 Democratic Party presidential candidates, 2016

Name	Current/last political post	Announced (2015)	Exited (2015)
Hillary Clinton	Ex-Secretary of State	12 April	
Bernie Sanders	Senator (Vermont)	30 April	
Martin O'Malley	Ex-Governor (Maryland)	30 May	
Lincoln Chafee	Ex-Governor (Rhode Island)	3 June	23 October
Jim Webb	Ex-Senator (Virginia)	2 July	20 October

That left only Vermont senator Bernie Sanders, who can be best understood as the Corbyn-esque candidate — except that Sanders isn't even a member of the party he aspires to lead. He has spent 24 years in Congress as an independent, although he always sits with — and usually votes with — the Democrats. Sanders is a 74-year-old, slightly dishevelled activist-come-politician, who through his firebrand rhetoric and savvy use of social media appeals to the non-establishment wing of the Democratic Party. (You can see the Corbyn similarity.) He just might give Clinton a few early scares in Iowa and New Hampshire, but after that you can forget the Corbyn victory analogy.

The timetable

Table 6.3 shows the Democratic Party's nomination schedule — correct as at mid-November. The Iowa caucuses and New Hampshire primary are a month later than in 2012, but Super Tuesday (with over 1,000 delegates contested) remains as the first Tuesday in March. The third Tuesday of March sees a further nearly 800 delegates selected in five large states, and there's a regional primary around the mid-Atlantic states at the end of April.

Table 6.3 Democratic Party primary/caucus calendar, 2016

Date	State	Election type	Delegates
1 **February**	Iowa	Non-binding caucuses	52
9 February	New Hampshire	Modified primary	32
20 February	Nevada	Non-binding caucuses	43
27 February	South Carolina	Open primary	59
1 **March**	Alabama	Open primary	60
	Arkansas	Open primary	37
	Colorado	Non-binding caucuses	77
	Georgia	Open primary	112
	Massachusetts	Modified primary	116
	Minnesota	Caucuses	94
	Oklahoma	Closed primary	42
	Tennessee	Open primary	76
	Texas	Closed primary	252
	Vermont	Open primary	26
	Virginia	Open primary	110
5 March	Kansas	Caucuses	37
	Louisiana	Closed primary	61
	Nebraska	Non-binding caucuses	30
6 March	Maine	Non-binding caucuses	30
8 March	Michigan	Open primary	148
	Mississippi	Open primary	41

Table 6.3 Democratic Party primary/caucus calendar, 2016 (Continued)

Date	State	Election type	Delegates
15 March	Florida	Closed primary	246
	Illinois	Open primary	186
	Missouri	Open primary	84
	North Carolina	Modified primary	121
	Ohio	Modified primary	159
22 March	Arizona	Closed primary	85
	Idaho	Caucuses	27
	Utah	Caucuses	37
26 March	Alaska	Non-binding caucuses	20
	Hawaii	Caucuses	34
	Washington	Caucuses	118
5 **April**	Wisconsin	Open primary	89
9 April	Wyoming	Caucuses	17
19 April	New York	Closed primary	277
26 April	Connecticut	Closed primary	70
	Delaware	Closed primary	27
	Maryland	Closed primary	101
	Pennsylvania	Closed primary	181
	Rhode Island	Modified primary	31
3 **May**	Indiana	Open primary	80
10 May	West Virginia	Modified primary	33
17 May	Kentucky	Closed primary	53
	Oregon	Closed primary	64
7 **June**	California	Modified primary	476
	Montana	Open primary	22
	New Jersey	Modified primary	126
	New Mexico	Closed primary	38
	North Dakota	Caucuses	19
	South Dakota	Modified primary	20
14 June	District of Columbia	Closed primary	43

Note: Total number of delegates: 4,764 (correct as of 19 November 2015), therefore the number of delegate votes required for nomination: 2,383.

The Republicans

Just too many candidates

By contrast, in the Republican corner things look somewhat over-crowded. By the end of July 2015, there were 17 declared candidates (see Table 6.4), easily a record for either party. It's the most bizarre list of names ever seen in a presidential race and far too many to comment on individually here.

Table 6.4 Republican Party presidential candidates, 2016

Name	Current/last political post	Announced (2015)	Exited (2015)
Ted Cruz	Senator (Texas)	23 March	
Rand Paul	Senator (Kentucky)	7 April	
Marco Rubio	Senator (Florida)	13 April	
Ben Carson	[none]	3 May	
Carly Fiorina	[none]	4 May	
Mike Huckabee	Ex-Governor (Arkansas)	5 May	
Rick Santorum	Ex-Senator (Pennsylvania)	27 May	
George Pataki	Ex-Governor (New York)	28 May	
Lindsey Graham	Senator (South Carolina)	1 June	
Rick Perry	Ex-Governor (Texas)	4 June	11 September
Jeb Bush	Ex-Governor (Florida)	15 June	
Donald Trump	[none]	16 June	
Bobby Jindal	Ex-Governor (Louisiana)	24 June	17 November
Chris Christie	Governor (New Jersey)	30 June	
Scott Walker	Governor (Wisconsin)	13 July	21 September
John Kasich	Governor (Ohio)	21 July	
Jim Gilmore	Ex-Governor (Virginia)	30 July	

Three possible scenarios

So how will the Republican nomination race develop? As I write this in the autumn of 2015, there would appear to be three possible scenarios. Let's take them from the least to the slightly more likely. Surprisingly, the least likely scenario seems to be that one of the Republicans' traditional insider candidates will eventually win the day. But this is what happened in 2008 when the party nominated John McCain, who was virtually dead in the water only weeks before the primaries began. So, under this scenario, the party would nominate someone like Jeb Bush, John Kasich or Chris Christie — a well-known, long-standing insider. After all, it's what the Republican Party usually does.

Scenario number 2 is that one of the non-traditional outsiders is chosen. Donald Trump and Ben Carson have been the front-runners in the polls right through the Invisible Primary. Although both of them are outsiders, that's all they have in common. Trump is loud, brash, usually out of control, appeals to less religious, blue-collar Republicans and speaks as if he's addressing fourth graders. Carson is quiet, controlled and low key, and appeals to conservative, white-collar, evangelical voters. Both are drawing their appeal from the many in the party who

are turned off their Republican politicians in Washington and beyond, and who are looking for a complete outsider.

Scenario 3 goes something like this. Trump and Carson implode as Republicans realise that neither of them can beat Hillary Clinton, but none of the traditional insiders manages to emerge from the pack. Republican voters then turn to an outsider-insider and find Marco Rubio, or possibly Ted Cruz. Certainly the 44-year-old Rubio would make a very good foil for the 69-year-old Clinton. Which, if any, of these scenarios plays out will probably have become clear by Super Tuesday.

The timetable

Table 6.5 shows the Republican Party's nomination schedule — correct as at early November. (Most states have scheduled the Republican and Democratic contests on the same day.) The Republican state parties have been much better in 2016 at sticking to the national party's rules. In both the last two cycles, some states scheduled primaries before permitted dates and were penalised by a reduction in their delegate allocation. This year, however, all the state parties — including Florida — have obeyed the national rules, including the one that forbids any winner-take-all primaries before 15 March.

Table 6.5 Republican Party primary/caucus calendar, 2016

Date	State	Election type	Delegates
1 **February**	Iowa	Caucuses	30
9 February	New Hampshire	Modified primary	23
20 February	South Carolina	Open primary	50
23 February	Nevada	Caucuses	30
1 **March**	Alabama	Open primary	50
	Alaska	Caucuses	28
	Arkansas	Open primary	40
	Colorado	Non-binding caucuses	37
	Georgia	Modified primary	76
	Massachusetts	Modified primary	42
	Minnesota	Caucuses	38
	Oklahoma	Closed primary	43
	Tennessee	Open primary	58
	Texas	Open primary	155
	Vermont	Open primary	16
	Virginia	Open primary	49
	Wyoming	Non-binding caucuses	29

Table 6.5 Republican Party primary/caucus calendar, 2016 (Continued)

Date	State	Election type	Delegates
5 March	Kansas	Caucuses	40
	Kentucky	Caucuses	45
	Louisiana	Closed primary	46
	Maine	Caucuses	23
8 March	Hawaii	Caucuses	19
	Idaho	Closed primary	32
	Michigan	Closed primary	59
	Mississippi	Open primary	39
12 March	District of Columbia	Caucuses	19
15 March	Florida*	Closed primary	99
	Illinois	Open primary	69
	Missouri	Modified primary	52
	North Carolina	Modified primary	72
	Ohio	Modified primary	66
22 March	Arizona*	Closed primary	58
	Utah	Non-binding caucuses	40
1–3 **April**	North Dakota	State convention	28
5 April	Wisconsin	Open primary	42
19 April	New York	Closed primary	95
26 April	Connecticut	Closed primary	28
	Delaware*	Closed primary	16
	Maryland	Closed primary	38
	Pennsylvania	Closed primary	71
	Rhode Island	Modified primary	19
3 **May**	Indiana	Open primary	57
10 May	Nebraska	Modified primary	36
	West Virginia	Modified primary	34
17 May	Oregon	Closed primary	28
24 May	Washington	Closed primary	44
7 **June**	California	Closed primary	172
	Montana	Closed primary	27
	New Jersey*	Modified primary	51
	New Mexico	Closed primary	24
	South Dakota	Closed primary	29

* holding winner-take-all primary

Note: Total number of delegates: 2,472 (correct as of 19 November 2015), therefore number of delegate votes required for nomination: 1,237.

The types of contest

Tables 6.3 and 6.5 show the different types of contest being held during the 2016 nomination cycle. Here's a quick run-down on these different types of contest:

- **Primary:** a state-based election to choose a party's presidential candidate. A presidential primary shows support for a candidate among ordinary voters and often also chooses delegates committed to vote for that candidate at the national party convention.
- **Caucuses:** a state-based series of meetings to choose a party's candidate for the presidency. They fulfil the same functions as primaries. In 2016, around one quarter of states will use caucuses.
- **Open primary:** a primary in which any registered voter can vote in the primary of either party.
- **Closed primary:** a primary in which only registered Republicans can vote in the Republican primary, and only registered Democrats can vote in the Democratic primary.
- **Modified primary:** a primary in which registered Republicans can vote only in the Republican primary, and registered Democrats can vote only in the Democratic primary, but those registered as independents may vote in either party's primary.
- **Non-binding primary/caucus:** a primary/caucus in which delegates are not selected — that is, the delegates chosen are not bound by the result of the primary/caucus. This is also referred to as a 'beauty contest' or 'preference vote'.
- **Winner-take-all primary:** a primary in which the winner of the primary is awarded all that state's delegates. Democrats do not permit winner-take-all primaries. Even amongst Republicans, they are now a dying breed: only four states (Arizona, Delaware, Florida and New Jersey) are holding winner-take-all primaries in 2016.
- **Proportional primary:** a primary in which delegates are awarded in proportion to the votes that each candidate wins. Most states set a threshold — a minimum percentage of votes that a candidate must receive to get any of the state's delegates, usually set at 15% of the vote. All Democratic primaries are proportional primaries.

The conventions and debates

Being the challenging party, the Republicans will be the first of the major parties to hold their convention. That's a long-standing tradition. For their venue, the Republicans have chosen Cleveland, Ohio. This will be the first Republican convention in the city for 80 years. Not only have the Republicans chosen an unusual venue, but they will hold their earliest convention since 1980, gathering in Cleveland on 18–21 July.

The Democrats will gather in Philadelphia on 25–28 July, the week after the Republicans have concluded their convention, making this the earliest Democratic convention since 1992. They last held their convention in Philadelphia back in 1948. The Democrats have announced a significant reduction in the number of delegates attending the convention in 2016 — of around 800 — maybe another indication that the parties are wanting to scale back their conventions in an era when their significance and relevance are being questioned.

The 2016 presidential debates will take place on 26 September, 9 October and 19 October, with the vice presidential debate on 4 October.

Questions

1 Why did Vice President Joe Biden decide against running for the presidency in 2016?
2 What strengths does Hillary Clinton have in the 2016 Democratic nomination race? What weaknesses might hinder her campaign?
3 What similarities does the author see between Bernie Sanders and UK Labour Party leader Jeremy Corbyn?
4 The author has outlined three possible scenarios for the Republican nomination race in 2016. Which, if any, do you think has actually played out? Give your reasons.
5 Briefly explain the different types of presidential primary that will be held in 2016.